Seeing Differently

Finding God in all creation, in suffering people, in caring for the drains, in poetry and singing, even in 'Sister Death': this book is an inspiration and an education not only in seeing but also in living differently in our century that so desperately needs Franciscan wisdom. It draws readers into a liberating, transformative penitence that is about 'a lifetime of change' for the sake of more and more loving – of God, God's creation, and each other.

David Ford
Regius Professor of Divinity Emeritus
University of Cambridge

Francis of Assisi was a nature mystic but his path to solidarity with creation began in prayer and opening his heart to God. In this book, the power of vision is emphasized as the portal between the inner world and the outer world: Francis learned to see because he learned to love. It brings to mind the insight of another great Franciscan mystic, Angela of Foligno, who wrote: "As we see, so we love and the more perfectly and purely we see, the more perfectly and purely we love." Learning to see differently is the beginning of a new social order, a new planetary community, where love of God, love of neighbour and love of all creatures creates a new house, a new church, built on the foundation of a new heart. This wonderful book is a helpful guide toward creating a new world.

Sr Ilia Delio, OSF
Connelly Chair in Theology
Villanova University

This is exactly the sort of book which we need at this moment in history. The pandemic has conspired with the distress of our young people and with Pope Francis, among many others, to make us aware of our disastrous impact on creation and our great need for the wisdom of St Francis of Assisi. Now three Franciscans have drawn together their own reflections and insights to share the sensitive prayer and tough thinking which echo Francis' own teaching. Like all good Franciscan history, the book begins with stories, and then gradually leads us deeper, until even the complexities of John Duns Scotus' essential but subtle thinking are woven into this rich heritage.

To recognize what is happening to our world requires a commitment not only to attention but to place. After *Laudato Si'*, this is the best Franciscan reflection on the crisis of our planet that I have read, and I very much hope many others will read it, take it to heart and join the growing movement of those who are trying to listen, before it is too late, to the voice of our suffering Sister Mother Earth.

Sr Frances Teresa Downing OSC

Seeing Differently

Franciscans and Creation

Simon Cocksedge, Samuel Double
and Nicholas Alan Worssam

CANTERBURY
PRESS
Norwich

© Simon Cocksedge, Samuel Double, Nicholas Alan Worssam 2021

Published in 2021 by Canterbury Press
Editorial office
3rd Floor, Invicta House,
108–114 Golden Lane,
London EC1Y 0TG, UK
www.canterburypress.co.uk

Canterbury Press is an imprint of Hymns Ancient & Modern Ltd
(a registered charity)

Hymns Ancient & Modern® is a registered trademark of
Hymns Ancient & Modern Ltd
13A Hellesdon Park Road, Norwich,
Norfolk NR6 5DR, UK

Rainer Maria Rilke, Selected Poems, translations © Susan Ranson and
Marielle Sutherland 2011. Reproduced with permission of the Licensor,
Oxford University Press, through PLSclear.

David Scott's poem 'A Long Way from Bread' from Beyond the
Drift: New and Selected Poems, 2015, reproduced by permission of
Bloodaxe Books.

Scripture quotations are from New Revised Standard Version Bible:
Anglicized Edition, copyright © 1989, 1995 National Council of the
Churches of Christ in the United States of America. Used by permission.
All rights reserved worldwide.

British Library Cataloguing in Publication data

A catalogue record for this book is available
from the British Library

978-1-78622-300-5

Typeset by Regent Typesetting

Contents

So if anyone is in Christ, there is a new creation: everything old has passed away; see, everything has become new! All this is from God, who reconciled us to himself through Christ, and has given us the ministry of reconciliation; that is, in Christ God was reconciling the world to himself. (2 Cor. 5.17–19)

A certain member of what was then considered the circle of the wise once approached the just Anthony and asked him 'How do you ever manage to carry on, Father, deprived as you are of the consolation of books?' His reply: 'My book, sir philosopher, is the nature of created things, and it is always at hand when I wish to read the words of God.' (Evagrius Ponticus, p. 39)

'Please concentrate on creation ... and ignore the destruction around us.' *Doctor's words to pregnant mother delivering by candlelight during a bombing raid.* (Nichol, p. 89)

We are intimately interconnected with nature, whether we like it or not. If we don't take care of nature, we can't take care of ourselves. (United Nations Environment Programme Executive Director, Inger Andersen)

Acknowledgements

The three authors – Simon, Nick and Sam – have cooperated closely on this Franciscan project, not only through their own contributions but in critiquing and advising upon the writing of one another. There's something of each one of us that runs throughout, so we share responsibility for the book as a whole. We give thanks for one another's inspiration and for our friendship which has been deepened by the venture. The fact that much of the work has been accomplished while 'locked down' on account of the Covid-19 pandemic has involved a particular challenge. We are grateful for the interconnectedness made possible by Zoom.

We are also very grateful to Stephanie Cloete, Sally Cocksedge, Elizabeth Cook, John-Francis Friendship, Bob Gilbert, Nick Sagovsky, Christine Smith and Patrick Woodhouse, and everyone at St Leonard's in Assisi for commenting on drafts, along with general advice and support throughout this project.

Foreword

We live in a time of rapid change and great challenge, seemingly coming at us faster because of the coronavirus pandemic and its economic consequences. The reality of climate change and environmental degradation is also upon us because we human beings have lived as if this world is ours to use and consume rather than to serve and conserve. Sometimes a crisis paralyses us. What can I do when the forces upon me are so great and any action I could take so insignificant? But a crisis is both a judgement in which we see things more clearly *and* an opportunity to turn things round and do things differently.

We are beginning to see things differently. To do this creatively needs wisdom and the religions of the world have much to offer. Within Christianity the tradition that has grown from the life of St Francis is particularly rich and fertile. This book has grown out of a renewal of that tradition within the Anglican Communion. Our Roman Catholic brothers and sisters are engaged in a similar process under the leadership of Pope Francis. His hugely influential environmental letter *Laudato Si'*, on care for our common home, was addressed not just to Roman Catholics, or Christians, or the world's faiths, or people of good will but to everyone on this resilient, fragile, creative planet earth.

Every bishop is grateful for good news and good news that renews hope is often hard won. I have known the Society of St Francis for nearly all my adult life. I first visited Hilfield in Dorset, in the Diocese of Salisbury where I am now the bishop, as a student. It is a beautiful place, nestled beneath the steep slope of Batcombe Down, which the Franciscans make available to guests. There is a lovely spirit of joyful, prayerful, inclusive simplicity in which prayer keeps the imagination alive. The same spirit animates the other Franciscan houses I have known in Alnmouth, Whitechapel, Plaistow, Scunthorpe, Cambridge, Canterbury, Birmingham, and in their wonderfully contemplative house at Glasshampton.

In recent years, the community at Hilfield decided to make a simple, small and utterly demanding change of direction by addressing issues of the environment and the care of God's creation. What does it mean to live sustainably and how might we do this in such a way as to help heal the earth? The direction of travel was well set before I became bishop, nearly ten years ago, but it has been wonderfully sustained and developed. It is deeply local and it is world class.

Seeing Differently is an encouraging story of giving things up and new ways emerging from the old. By concentrating not on the needs of the community, but on the development of a way of life which treads lightly and creatively on God's earth, the Society of St Francis at Hilfield attracts people who want to learn with them and work alongside them for a period. Paradoxically, as an unintended consequence and a striking example of losing and finding, the religious community of SSF has gained new vocations and the Church has gained new committed lay people and priests.

In the UK, the early impact of the global coronavirus pandemic was first felt in 2020 as the days lengthened into a glorious spring and early summer. Reduced travel pollution brightened the sunlight and freshened the air. We rediscovered localism with heightened awareness of earth's beauty. Now, at the end of the year, with the longest dark nights and shortest days, a programme of mass vaccination has just begun. We dare to hope the overall impact of the pandemic will recede. Nevertheless, the economic effects will be with us for a long time. This is not being experienced equally: the poorest are having the hardest time.

If we can begin to see differently, this interesting and unique moment in time offers us an opportunity to live differently with an altered awareness of our world: the old order has become unsettled. There are now significant possibilities for us to think again about what it means to be human, the way we choose to live, and how we use the gifts of God's creation. *Seeing Differently*, a book by three Franciscans, could not be more timely. It is also a delight to read.

Think and pray it quietly but I dare to hope that the charism of St Francis to care for the environment might also have the unintended consequence of fulfilling his calling to rebuild the Church.

Nicholas Holtam, Bishop of Salisbury
Advent 2020

Seeing Differently

Learning to see differently

'I can say with some confidence that we are standing in one of the finest wildflower meadows in Dorset.' It was June 1995, and a Dorset Countryside Ranger was visiting to help us think through the problem of what to do about our land. The 19 acres of fields and woodland on the edge of the Dorset Downs had been part of the Franciscan friary at Hilfield for more than 70 years but were now becoming difficult to manage.

None of the brothers had any experience in farming and, to be honest, few had much interest in 'nature'. So looking after this bit of countryside, along with maintaining the life of the friary with its rhythm of daily prayer, welcoming guests, and caring for and repairing the old farm buildings, had been fairly low on our list of priorities. For most of the year this field stood empty and unappreciated, except by the families and young people who came to camp for two holiday weeks each summer. It was always a headache to get the long grass cut and cleared away before the campers' arrival.

Mid-June was a good time of year to be overlooking the meadow for it was thick with orchids. There was an abundance of Common Spotted Orchid, their pale pink flower heads reaching above surrounding grass, but also seven other varieties: Twayblade, Bee, Fly, Butterfly, Southern Marsh and Pyramid, with waxy Birds-nest Orchid in the hedgerow. This field had ideal conditions for these delicate flowers: thin, chalky, well-drained soil, which had been left 'unimproved' by fertilizer or selective weedkiller ever since the brothers had arrived in the 1920s. 'You have here', said the Ranger, 'a treasure to be guarded and nurtured.'

These words were a moment of re-vision. Not only did they begin a transformation in our Hilfield community's attitude towards our surroundings, with a refocusing on living wisely and gently within them, they also brought about a re-evaluation of our Franciscan vocation. Inadvertently, we were taught to see differently in the place that we were already inhabiting.

Of course, we knew about Francis of Assisi's joy in the natural world, such as stories of his special relationship with creatures great and small, and his Canticle of the Creatures. But the application of all this was limited to agreeing, often rather reluctantly, to speak at occasional pet services. There was little recognition that ecology had much to do with the main focus of our mission and ministry, which was in cities among those on society's margins and in working for justice and peace.

Since then, however, Hilfield Friary has become a centre of conservation and sustainability, and a home to a community of men and women, young and old, married and single who live and work alongside the brothers in caring for creation. Neighbouring fields have been acquired to recover them as wildflower meadows, livestock have been introduced to graze them carefully, fruit and vegetable gardens have been developed, and an attention to food and its sourcing has been established. Solar and carbon-neutral energy has replaced dependence on gas, and buildings have been heavily insulated. The friary was the first institution in the UK to be given an Eco-Church Gold Award by A Rocha UK, a Christian organization committed to promoting creation-care (see Hilfield Friary and A Rocha websites).

Inspired by the writing of Franciscan Leonardo Boff, the place is now a witness to an integrated ecology – environmental, social and spiritual – as an alternative to the crazily destructive contemporary way of life of which we are a part and for which we all share responsibility. Over the same period of time, and related to what has been happening at Hilfield, there has been a growing awareness among Franciscans in general that Francis' way of seeing creation, and the theology and spirituality that underlie it, contain a wealth of wisdom that is urgently needed in a market-driven and often nature-blind mind-set.

Our hope is that the 'seeing differently' offered in this book contributes to that wisdom and its application in reconciling human behaviour with today's world. We begin by retelling many of the stories about Francis himself and creation (Chapter 2), along with an exploration of the Canticle of the Creatures (Chapter 3). This song, written towards the end of his life, encapsulates his teaching regarding humanity's fellowship with the rest of creation. Chapter 4 outlines Francis' lived spirituality of creation. His followers' development of this spirituality over subsequent centuries is explored in Chapters 5, 6 and 7. Finally, with particular reference to Hilfield Friary and urban living in London, we share something of present-day Franciscans' experiences in relating to and living within creation (Chapters 8, 9 and 10).

Many people today fear that the creation around us 'is all being destroyed'. Our aim in this book is to 'concentrate on creation' through the eyes of Francis of Assisi, his followers over the years and contemporary Franciscans. Having engaged deeply with this topic, we are certain that Franciscan wisdom has a great deal of relevance for all of us as we face environmental breakdown with all its many frightening consequences. We hope to contribute to current debates about humanity's relationship with creation and ways in which we can avoid potential destruction. We also hope readers will be inspired to see differently and then to act on behalf of creation in their own lives. Such an outcome would be truly Franciscan!

Many factors have influenced this book. Below we highlight three: Francis himself, his historical significance and ourselves as authors.

How Francis came to see differently

As Franciscans, we are occasionally invited to speak at school assemblies. A good starting point is to ask pupils whether they have heard of or know anything about Francis of Assisi. Particularly if it is a church primary school, the chances are that hands will shoot up, and we know which answer is coming:

'He loved animals.' It's the one thing about St Francis that most children will be able to remember. That probably goes for their teachers too!

The stories of Francis preaching to birds and the wolf of Gubbio are well known and often illustrated in books about the saint. It's easy for people to relate to these and one can continue from there to speak about other aspects of his life; there might seem to be a progression from his being the most famous lover of animals to his being recognized as the patron saint of ecology. Yet making a connection between the Little Poor Man of Assisi and a Franciscan ecological wisdom for today, leaping the gap of 800 years, isn't quite so straightforward.

Francis grew up within and was shaped by an urban culture: he is identified by his city. But it was a very different kind of urban living from that which more than half the world's population experience today. Assisi in Francis' time was tiny and walled, with a population of between two and three thousand, nestling against a mountain range on one side and overlooking a valley of farmland and woods. Many citizens worked the land and all had small plots on which to grow vines, fruit and vegetables, raise pigs and keep hens for eggs. There was an intimate if often fragile connection between land and food, weather and work, animals and humans, a connection that is known to few people today. The natural environment of Francis' time was full of mystery and precariousness. Suffering and death were ever-present realities. Most diseases were incurable and life expectancy was short: Francis died aged 44 years.

Francis' turnaround from youth to saint (Vauchez, 2012, p. 19) took place in close contact with the natural world. Brought up in an affluent merchant household, he left home some six months after his second attempt to become a knight had failed in summer 1205. During those six months he stopped working in his father's cloth business and his behaviour became erratic. He wandered the local forests and spent time praying, often in caves in the hills or in churches and crypts near Assisi. His living conditions were poor and dirty and he lost weight; when, unkempt, he came into Assisi to beg for food and building materials, people treated him as insane.

It was not until early 1208 that other men began to join Francis and to form a brotherhood. During the intervening two years, records tell us that he begged for food, prayed and worked with his hands to restore small churches, especially San Damiano, a church just outside Assisi where he became resident in late 1205. They also note several key moments in Francis' spiritual journey that can be seen as affecting his relationship with creation. The precise historical order in which these events took place is uncertain, as the records, while often corroborating the reality of the events, vary in many details. This is discussed further in the Appendix.

Historians agree that a very significant turning point was an encounter with a leper (I.195). People with leprosy were seen as the least in society, living without health care in leper houses outside towns. Like everyone at the time, Francis had always avoided lepers, finding them repugnant. But one day while out riding, he met a leper and felt called to overcome his fears; he dismounted, kissed the man's hand, gave him money, and a few days later visited the leper house. After this, he regularly spent time there caring for residents. Near the end of his life, he wrote of how important this encounter had been in changing his attitudes: by showing mercy, love and compassion to these outcasts, Francis experienced God's transforming mercy and grace himself. Through rejected lepers, he came to recognize the presence of Christ in all human beings.

Another important early experience took place at the tumble-down church of San Damiano at the end of 1205. A large crucifix hung in the church: today it can be seen in St Clare's Basilica in Assisi. While he was praying, 'he heard with his bodily ears a voice coming from that cross, telling him three times: "Francis, go and repair my house which, as you see, is all being destroyed"' (II.536). Initially, Francis interpreted this as an instruction to repair ruined churches, of which there were many near Assisi. Later he came to realize it was more about repairing the whole Christian Church. Contemporary writers have added another interpretation: that the house in question is actually the whole of creation. Viewed this way, care and stewardship of creation, along with ensuring sustainability, have been integral to the Franciscan ideal from its earliest days.

Francis' growing desire to live in complete poverty, following the example of Jesus, was another influence. It led to the occasion, soon after hearing the voice from the cross at San Damiano and overseen by the Bishop of Assisi outside his residence, at which he publicly renounced his merchant father and his family riches in favour of his heavenly Father and poverty (I.193). This decision had many consequences, including shaping Francis' relationship with creation – away from possession, domination and power towards minority, fraternity, cooperation and reconciliation (see pp. 154–5).

The biblical example of Jesus was also important for Francis as his early vocation developed: there are several stories of his obedience to Gospel instructions during this time. In one version (I.201), he heard a reading of Matthew's Gospel describing Jesus sending his twelve disciples to proclaim the good news: 'Take no gold, or silver, or copper in your belts, no bag for your journey, or two tunics, or sandals, or a staff; for labourers deserve their food' (Matt. 10.9–10). Straight away Francis took off his shoes, made himself a rough tunic and exchanged his leather belt for a cord. 'Overflowing with joy', he 'hastened to implement the words of salvation' (I.202). We can see in this example how scriptural words inspired Francis to see and act differently, and shaped his relationship with created things. Off come belt and clothes, and on go a simple cord and single tunic. From that time on, Francis would not touch money.

These examples demonstrate some of the influences on young Francis as he matured into a holy man, closely in touch with the natural world surrounding him but fully aware, through living in extreme poverty, of creation's harsher side. Begging, building and praying, this initial stage of his journey must have been lonely, but from it emerged his desire to commit his life to drawing close to God through poverty, humility (from the Latin: *humus* meaning earth), simplicity and prayer. In the chapters that follow, we will explore Francis' relationship with creation in more detail.

Creation, Christian history and Francis

'The earth is the Lord's and all that is in it' (Ps. 24.1). So sings
the psalmist who strikes a note that runs throughout the Bible,
in the Hebrew Scriptures and the New Testament. The context
of the earth and our relationship with it is so obvious that it's
often overlooked, particularly as we tend to focus on the Scriptures as a series of stories about people and their relationship
with God. From the beginning, where Adam is created from
the earth's dust (Gen. 2.7), to the end, where the writer envis-
ages a 'new heaven and a new earth' (Rev. 21.1), the planet
out of which we are made is both setting and vehicle for God's
self-revelation. This revelation comes to wonderful fulfilment
in Jesus Christ's life, death and resurrection, 'The Word became
flesh and lived among us' (John 1.14). The Scriptures provide
the basis for Christian reflection on creation.

Origen, coming at the start of the third century, was one
of the earliest Christian writers in the extensive tradition of
thinking concerning creation. Although his work has over the
years been considered controversial, he had a great influence
on many who came after him. According to Origen, through
creating, the Word of God left signs of himself in the world
around us, created words that are immanent in things, inherent
in them:

> I think that He who made all things in wisdom so created
> all the species of visible things upon earth, that he placed in
> them some teaching and knowledge of things invisible and
> heavenly, whereby the human mind might mount to spiritual
> understanding and seek the grounds of things in heaven; so
> that taught by God's wisdom it might say: The things that
> are hid and that are manifest have I learned. (Origen, 1957,
> p. 220)

From sun, moon and stars to the smallest animals and plants,
all have details carrying the mark of the divine art and the
Lord's hand. In other words, all creation bears the Creator's
imprint and so all creation speaks of God.

St Augustine of Hippo, writing not long after Origen, could show God's works but not God: 'As we contemplate his works let us praise the worker, the maker for what is made, the creator for his creation, passing in review all the things known to us, things plain to see' (Augustine, 2004, p. 383).

Francis of Assisi belongs to a long line of Christian thinkers concerning creation from Augustine and Origen to the present day. In the twentieth century, for example, von Balthasar noted in his classic work on prayer:

> Christ gathers up in himself all the words of God lying scattered in the world ... not only the 'words spoken in many ways' of the Old Testament, but equally those scattered throughout creation, stammered or murmured in it – words uttered in the great and the small things of nature, the words of the flowers and the beasts, words of overpowering beauty and paralysing horror, words manifold and confused, this word full of promise and disillusionment of human existence – that all these belong to the one, eternal, living Word become man for us; they are wholly his property, and on that account are governed by him, to be interpreted by his light and no other. (Balthasar, 1961, p. 16)

Truly to see these words (Greek *logoi*) implanted by the Word (*Logos*) in ordinary things and everyday life is a lifetime's work. 'To be able to look steadily at, say, a bluebell or a kestrel, not distracted by anything, not even the associations of the flower or the bird, but to see it for itself as an expression of the divine creative Mind' is part of contemplation, 'a disinterested perception of things as creatively envisaged by God' (Nichols, 2019, p. 62).

Acquiring such dispassionate discernment has been part of spiritual training for centuries. Described by Evagrius in the fourth century, it was developed by St Benedict in the sixth century in writing the first monastic Rule of Life in the Western Church. Numerous writings since then, such as those of Julian of Norwich of the fourteenth-century English mystics and Teresa of Avila in sixteenth-century Spain, have been concerned with the relationship between creation, prayer and each soul's journey. The example and writings of Francis of Assisi are part of this lengthy story within Christian history, and they continue to inspire today.

The authors and this book

Any publication is limited by its authors' knowledge and experience. We are members of the Church of England's Society of St Francis (SSF), trying to live our Franciscan vocation in different ways in the United Kingdom in the early part of the twenty-first century. Samuel Double is a First Order brother who has long experience of a varied mendicant lifestyle. Nicholas Worssam, also a First Order brother, lives a semi-enclosed monastic life within the SSF family, not unlike that of Second Order sisters. Simon Cocksedge is a married member of the Third Order of the SSF (TSSF).

The richness of our experiences over many years (between us we have clocked up some 115 years as Franciscans at the time of writing) add to this work but we write from a UK, SSF and Anglican background. We are not academic theologians or historians. Despite this, we hope that our book, and the Franciscan example it offers, will challenge readers to revisit their own relationship with the wonder-full creation that we have been given to dwell in together. If our words enable you, our reader, to reread God's words and see creation differently then perhaps you might be enthused to pray and act differently too, to reconcile humanity within the great gift of God's creation. Such prayer and action are the foundations of following in the footsteps of St Francis of Assisi.

Brother Samuel

My Franciscan life began when I joined the First Order of the Society of St Francis in 1975 at Hilfield Friary in west Dorset, which nestles below the Dorset Downs' northern escarpment.

This is deep countryside with narrow lanes and high hedge-rows; cows outnumber people and our friary is four miles from a village. Originally known as Flowers Farm, it has been home to Anglican Franciscans since 1921 when three brothers, inspired by Francis' commitment to those on society's margins, arrived to set up a sanctuary for the many unemployed men tramping the roads after World War One.

The founders called those who came to them 'wayfaring brothers' and offered basic but gentle hospitality, training in various crafts, and the hope of a more dignified and secure future. The farm itself, in that time of agricultural depression, was never profitable and was soon separated from the friary, but a small amount of land was retained which provided work and some food for the community. The friary has changed a lot since 1975. There are fewer brothers, and homeless way-farers no longer stay there. Instead, others – men and women, married and single, younger and older – share the brothers' life in community, till and keep the land, care for guests and love the place.

Although the Franciscan life is itinerant or mendicant and 'the world's our cloister', Hilfield is the place to which, like a homing pigeon, I have kept returning over the years. I feel I know every brick, stone and flint of the buildings grouped around the original farmyard, along with the corners of every field and woodland and the plants that inhabit them. It seems like home. This is where I have learnt a 'care for the common home' of creation, out of which has developed a passionate concern for ecology – a word whose root meaning is 'the wisdom of the household'.

Three years ago I moved to our Franciscan friary in Plaistow, east London. A Franciscan witness has been long established here in what was traditionally an area serving London's dock-lands and associated industries. It is now vibrantly multicultural: shops selling food and goods from around the world overflow onto pavements. There are Pentecostal churches established in redundant cinemas, and close to our house a pub has been con-verted into an Islamic centre and madrasa. Not far away are two large Sikh gurdwaras and a golden Hindu temple.

The area suffers from many of the problems of poor urban centres of population in London and around the world. Depleted public services due to years of austerity combine with inadequate and insufficient housing. The borough of Newham, in which Plaistow is set, has the highest housing waiting list of any borough nationally. Development is all around us as London expands into every unused space; we are surrounded by cranes and concrete, transport is congested, roads are crowded and air quality often breaches safety levels.

It is very different from Dorset, but if you need to dwell in a city, London is not a bad place to live. There are some wonderful parks and open spaces, a free transport system for residents over 65, and great opportunities for enjoying culture, sport, and every kind of social engagement.

I came to live here partly because I felt that I needed to move on from Hilfield, for my own and for the friary's sake. But partly also because I was often challenged by those who told me that a care for creation was all very well for those living in the countryside or leafy suburbs, but was hardly a priority for those in cities. I wanted to respond to this challenge, reflect on it and investigate an urban as well as a rural ecology, particularly because Franciscans have traditionally tended to establish their friaries in towns. As someone deeply committed to following the example of Francis of Assisi, what I write explores how I am learning to see creation differently through the inherent contrasts between community life in rural west Dorset and urban east London.

Brother Nicholas Alan

Some 30 years ago, when I was in my mid-twenties, I visited Glasshampton Monastery in Worcestershire for the first time. I had already been to Hilfield Friary in Dorset a few times, and was keen to experience a more contemplative side of the Franciscan tradition. Just finding the monastery was, and still is, a fairly major expedition. Buses run every two hours, sometimes according to the timetable, weaving through the villages, and dropping you off at a turning onto a farm track. A sign greets the weary traveller: 'Wulstans Farm and Glasshampton Monastery – No entry for Motor Vehicles', as if motor vehicles were a new and unwanted invention to be abandoned as soon as possible. Actually, the sign is something of a warning, as the way up to the monastery is pitted with potholes and ruts, sometimes more of a river than a road. But public transport is still the best way to arrive, as the mile-long track up the hill acts as a kind of decompression chamber for those slowly emerging from the deep waters of the cities into the oxygen-rich air of Glasshampton hill.

The house itself is 200 years old, a former stable block attached to a mansion that burned to the ground almost as soon as it had been built. The bedrooms of the monastery were once horse boxes, the chapel a carriage house with hayloft over. One hundred years ago a member of the Society of the Divine Compassion, Father William Sirr, left his busy ministry in the East End of London, in the house in Plaistow where Brother Samuel now lives, to begin a more contemplative community along the lines of an Anglican Cistercian monastery. People came and went, but none stayed, perhaps due to the cold and damp, the poor food and the long hours of prayer in the chapel day and night. Eventually William had to leave without achieving his dream, but ten years later the Society of St Francis was offered the property as a place to train its novices, giving them a taste of a hermitage within the Franciscan tradition, in many ways the equivalent of the Second Order of contemplative women founded by Clare of Assisi, Francis' great friend.

My own year here as a novice was sandwiched between a year at Hilfield Friary and a year in Birmingham in a council house on an outer rim estate. Three rather breathless years of great contrasts and constant lessons to be learned. Then three years exploring the hermit life with one other brother, before returning to Glasshampton Monastery to pray, study and work. Prior to joining the SSF I had spent three years in Korea, teaching English and supporting the English-language ministry at the Anglican Cathedral in downtown Seoul. It was a precious time to discover that there is only one human race and that we are all brothers and sisters in a vast extended family.

Since joining the Society of St Francis in 1995 I have spent around 20 years here at Glasshampton as a member of the community. Like Brother Samuel's love of Hilfield, I feel a great affection for this place that I have been privileged to call home. I know intimately the cascading slate roofs and the delicately arched brick lintels, the calls of the birds and the swaying of the silver birch in the wind, the smell of the wisteria and of the rich dark earth when it is ploughed in the fields around us. Sometimes when I am hundreds of miles away I wake and hear the Glasshampton turret clock sound the hours, or the angelus bell calling the brothers to their prayers.

Of course, the Franciscan brothers living here are all a part of the local habitat, participants in the vast interconnected web of creation. The vegetables we grow, albeit not so many now, and the apples we harvest, become part of our bodies; and the psalms and hymns we sing become part of our minds. Living, working and praying together seven days a week, we join the one great ecosystem of Glasshampton Monastery, within the continuous re-creation of the body of Christ.

If the monastery is to some extent enclosed, circling the inner space of a mossy green lawn, then prayer is the key that opens the gate into the inner, secret garden of our hearts. Returning every few hours to the chapel, we recite and listen to God's holy Word; returning throughout the day to the whispered love of God, we seek in prayer and service to share in God's reconciling peace.

Simon Cocksedge

Hilfield Friary, Glasshampton Monastery and following the Franciscan way through SSF have been part of my journey in life. I joined the Third Order in my teens having met brothers while at school and visited Hilfield in my gap year. I returned again as a student, and as a parent of young children enjoyed the ten days of the Hilfield Families Camp for more than

20 summers. My car automatically knows the route to Glass-hampton and I have visited with my family so many times over the years.

As a family doctor, I have served one community near Manchester for over 30 years. Living and working in this small town has enabled a deep knowledge of and respect for its people, from whom I have learnt so much and in whom I regularly catch glimpses of our divine Creator. Like Agatha Christie's Miss Marple at St Mary Mead, engaging deeply with one small corner of creation has made visible many facets of human existence over the years: psychological, spiritual and social as well as physical. For example, along with bodily illness, a family doctor's everyday work often involves exploring deep questions. These might be fears of never waking up following an upcoming general anaesthetic, or consequences from relationship breakdown: 'What does it all mean? Why is it like this? Why can't I just be happy?'

The Franciscan Third Order was set up by Francis himself in about 1212 for people who wished to follow his way but were unable to join the fraternity due to family or work commitments. Members commit to an individual rule of life which includes service through work, family or volunteering, annual retreat and daily prayer, study, and simplicity in living, along with regularly seeing a spiritual guide. The framework and stability arising from this rule, along with the guidance of an experienced pastor, have been integral to my engagement with people and place locally and to my spiritual journey.

In particular, my core vocation to prayer has underpinned marriage, family and professional life, along with my current work as a parish priest and hospice chaplain. Archbishop Michael Ramsey famously wrote that priests are called to soak themselves in prayer so they can be before God with the people on their hearts and before the people with God on their hearts (Ramsey, 1972, p. 14). I hope I have been able to embody something of that throughout my working life, following the prayerful example of Francis of Assisi.

We live surrounded by hills. They form a defining aspect of this small part of creation that I have come to know so well.

Walking their familiar footpaths is both relaxing and prayerful. It allows body, mind and spirit to recharge and refresh in the presence of God the Creator. Like Glasshampton, Hilfield, and our village church, these local hills are a thin spot, where the gap between heaven and earth is narrowed: England and nowhere, never and always, where prayer is valid. Praise God.

Questions for reflection

- Which aspects of the life of Francis of Assisi do you find helpful and why?
- How might a rule of life contribute to your personal journey?
- What would help you to see differently concerning your vocation or your relationship with creation?

Further reading

Susan Pitchford, 2006, *Following Francis: The Franciscan Way for Everyone*, Harrisburg, PA: Morehouse Publishing.

Augustine Thompson, 2012, *Francis of Assisi: A New Biography*, London: Cornell.

André Vauchez, 2012, *Francis of Assisi: The Life and Afterlife of a Medieval Saint*, London: Yale University Press.

Francis and Creation

SIMON COCKSEDGE

2

Francis and Creation: Stories

On entering 'Francis of Assisi images' into an internet search engine, you may not be surprised to learn that your results will be dominated by pictures of Francis with animals of some kind. Predominantly these tend to be birds but other possibilities include sheep, rabbits and a wolf. This is also true of the products sold in Assisi's many souvenir shops.

Scattered around Assisi are numerous statues of Francis. These are generally life-size and they portray very varied images. Animal accompaniment is much less frequent than in internet search pictures. Perhaps the most concentrated collection of statues of Francis and creatures is at the Papal Basilica of St Mary of the Angels, some four kilometres west of Assisi. Walking through the adjacent garden and cloister, you come across three statues in quick succession. One is of Francis tending a lamb, the next shows him holding a basket in which live doves regularly make their nest, and finally he leans against a wall intently studying a cicada (a cricket or grasshopper) on his finger.

All these images are based on stories in the Franciscan literature. They undoubtedly reflect the idealized picture in many people's minds of Francis as the idyllic 'patron saint of animals', always concerned for their well-being. Interestingly, Francis himself, outside the Rule, only mentions animals five times in his own writings. These focus instead on prayer and God's praise along with letters and instructions for his community of brothers.

In this chapter, most recorded stories about Francis and creation are either told or mentioned. They are, of course, numerous and are brought together to demonstrate the breadth of material in the literature. Some of the stories have been added to over the years by followers of Francis to establish his credentials as a great saint: this process is called hagiography and is considered in the Appendix. Nevertheless, all these stories contain truth: they can help us to begin to leave behind idealized or idyllic images and investigate Francis' real relationship with creation along with his underlying motivations. Such exploration in this chapter then informs discussion of Francis' spirituality of creation in Chapter 4.

Birds

Accounts about Francis and birds are the most numerous creation stories. They offer examples of various aspects of his relationships with animals. One story portrays Francis quietening some noisy swallows at Alviano. As local villagers silently awaited his sermon, nesting swallows noisily chirped so that Francis could not be heard. He asked the birds to quietly listen to the word of the Lord. Immediately, they fell silent and did not move until Francis finished talking (I.235).

We are not told that this sermon was *to* the swallows. In fact it reads as if the sermon was clearly to the people present but that the swallows were required to listen obediently. As a result, those listening wondered, marvelled and praised God. Additionally, Francis called the swallows 'sister', a title we might have thought was reserved for people. Its use points to the depth of his relationship with all animals and with all creation.

This story can be seen beautifully captured by Giotto in Assisi's Basilica of St Francis (Upper Church). It emphasizes key Franciscan themes: obedience; preaching resulting in listeners being led to worship God in praise; and Francis' loving relationship with both people and animals.

A second account may be another version of the same episode but with significant differences. This time Francis preached directly to a group of doves and crows near Bevagna. When he saw them, he ran in their direction:

They awaited him, [and] he greeted them in his usual way. He was quite surprised, however, because the birds did not take flight, as they usually do. Filled with great joy, he humbly requested that they listen to the word of God.

Among many other things, he said to them: 'My brother birds, you should greatly praise your Creator, and love Him always. He gave you feathers to wear, wings to fly, and whatever you need. God made you noble among His creatures and gave you a home in the purity of the air, so that, though you neither sow nor reap, He nevertheless protects and governs you without your least care.' He himself, and those brothers who were with him, used to say that, at these words, the birds rejoiced in a wonderful way according to their nature. They stretched their necks, spread their wings, opened their beaks and looked at him. He passed through their midst, coming and going, touching their heads and bodies with his tunic. Then he blessed them, and having made the sign of the cross, gave them permission to fly off to another place...

After the birds had listened so reverently to the word of God, he began to accuse himself of negligence because he had not preached to them before. From that day on, he carefully exhorted all birds, all animals, all reptiles, and also insensible creatures, to praise and love the Creator. (I.234)

Perhaps for the first time, but not for the last, Francis felt called to preach directly to members of the animal world other than human beings. His spontaneous enthusiasm in 'running swiftly' with 'great fervour' towards the birds echoes other instances when he began an action immediately, without pause for reflection or time to change his mind (e.g. II.623–4). His preaching, as so often, was of loving and praising God for all God's gifts, seen as pure grace, freely given to birds as to all people, including us. Francis, with great joy, initially asked the birds to listen and finally blessed them with the sign of the cross, before giving them permission to leave. Joyfulness and giving blessings are recurring themes throughout Francis' life, as are accessible and memorably enthusiastic preaching.

In St Bonaventure's version of these stories (II.592–3) the

birds, while obediently quiet during the brothers' office, joined in worship by singing and praising God beforehand and afterwards. This participation in worship and prayer occurs in other stories such as the cricket and a falcon that kept him company on a solitary retreat, helping with time-keeping:

> When blessed Francis, fleeing, as was his custom, from the sight of human company, came to stay in a certain hermitage place, a falcon nesting there bound itself to him in a great covenant of friendship. At night time with its calling and noise, it anticipated the hour when the saint would usually rise for the divine praises. The holy one of God was very grateful for this because the falcon's great concern for him shook him out of any sleeping-in. But when the saint was burdened more than usual by some illness, the falcon would spare him, and would not announce such early vigils. As if instructed by God, it would ring the bell of its voice with a light touch about dawn. (II.355)

Other birds offered welcome:

> When he went to the hermitage of La Verna to observe a forty-day fast in honour of the Archangel Michael, birds of different kinds flew around his cell, with melodious singing and joyful movements, as if rejoicing at his arrival. They seemed to be inviting and enticing the devoted father to stay. When he saw this, he said to his companion: 'I see, brother, that it is God's will that we stay here for some time, for our sisters the birds seem so delighted at our presence.' (II.593)

Larks were Francis' favourite bird. He probably saw a type of lark common in Italy variously called crested, hooded or 'cowled'. Francis interpreted the bird's cowl or hood as being like that worn by religious at that time. Francis noted Sister Lark's humility in looking for and eating food buried in manure and roadside waste, and in wearing plain brown plumage like a friar (II.130). He was inspired by larks singing, which he regarded as constantly praising God, like good religious. He also daydreamed of asking the Emperor to enact a law forbidding the trapping of larks and instructing that citizens should feed both poor people and all animals at Christmas.

Once again, we see Francis' ability to read sacramental symbolism into things he experienced in nature. God's creation spoke to him constantly of God, and all creation was sister or brother. This belief in fraternity and relationship among all creation had practical consequences. If all creation was equal then all creation should share in harvest fruits and be fed, whether poor or rich, bird, animal or human.

The same story (II.129) tells of larks circling where Francis lay, flying low and singing, on the evening that he died. The early accounts do not directly equate larks with angels singing at Francis' deathbed; nevertheless, that birds sing in mourning would have been a common thirteenth-century belief alongside that of angels accompanying souls to heaven (Armstrong, 1973, pp. 96–8). Thomas of Celano wondered 'whether [the larks on the evening of Francis' death] were showing their joy or their sadness with their song, we do not know. They sang with tearful joy and joyful tears, either to mourn the orphaned children, or to indicate the father's approach to eternal glory' (II.415). So mourning could be seen as turned to praise with larks as physical representations of the angelic host preparing to welcome Francis.

Another example of seeing Francis' relationship with creation through his interactions with birds is of a little water-bird:

> Blessed Francis was crossing the lake of Rieti in a small boat. A fisherman offered him a little water-bird ... The blessed Father received it gladly, and with open hands, gently invited it to fly away freely. But the bird ... settled down in his hands as in a nest, and the saint, his eyes lifted up, remained in prayer. Returning to himself, ... he sweetly told the little bird to return to its original freedom. And so the bird, having received permission with a blessing, flew away. (II.355)

Incidents involving saints handling or saving animals, which then refuse to depart, are common (Thompson, 2012, p. 224).

Other examples include rabbits reluctant to leave after being held in the saint's lap (I.235), a pheasant given to Francis while he was sick that would not leave him (II.356), doves rescued from a small boy selling them and then living in nests made by Francis (III.485), and fish:

> When he had the chance he would throw back into the water live fish that had been caught, and he warned them to be careful not to be caught again. One time while he was sitting in a little boat, ... a fisherman caught a large fish ... and reverently offered it to him. He accepted it gladly and gratefully, calling it 'brother'. He put it back in the water next to the little boat, and with devotion blessed the name of the Lord. For some time that fish did not leave the spot but stayed next to the boat, playing in the water where he put it until, at the end of his prayer, the holy man of God gave it permission to leave. (I.235)

Although some of these stories may be exaggerated, they demonstrate recurring themes in Francis' relationship with animals. First, they inspired him to prayer and were often depicted as staying alongside him as he prayed; second, they obediently would not depart without his permission; and last, Francis frequently gave them a blessing. This was his usual fraternal way of parting from any of his brothers or sisters, whether human or animal. These examples also suggest that in Francis' eyes, relationships with people were not distinguishable from those with animals. All were brothers and sisters within creation. But both humans and animals could behave poorly, as can be seen in two stories of Francis and birds.

Roger of Wendover, an English contemporary of Francis, recorded that Rome's citizens refused to accept Francis' preaching (I.599). He told them: 'to your shame I am going to preach the Good News of Christ to the wild animals and the birds of the air, that they might listen to the healing words of God, obey them, and find peace'. In the outskirts of Rome, he found crows, kites, magpies and other birds sitting among carrion. At Francis' command, they all silently listened attentively to his preaching. After three days of this, the Romans 'went out and with great veneration led the man of God back into the city'.

Previous bird encounters have felt joyous and celebratory, often with songbirds serenading or rejoicing with Francis. Outside Rome it was different: the mood desolate, the recipients the bird world's scavengers, feeding on carrion and often stealing young from other birds or animals. So Francis reprimanded the citizens of Italy's greatest city both directly verbally and indirectly through attending to, and being given attention by, these birds of destruction, the bird world's 'low-life'. This was not about celebrating or enjoying the animal kingdom but about shaming human beings.

The second example of poor behaviour concerns a greedy robin whose family had been feeding on crumbs at the brothers' table:

The young birds ... all ate together peacefully. But greed broke up this harmony, for a bigger one grew arrogant and harassed the smaller ones. When the big one had already eaten his fill, he still pushed the others away from the food. 'Look now,' said the father [Francis], 'at what this greedy one is doing! He's full to bursting, but he's still jealous of his hungry brothers. He will die an evil death.' The punishment followed soon after the saint's word. The one who disturbed his brothers climbed on the edge of a water pitcher to take a drink, and suddenly fell into it and drowned. (II.279)

These two stories suggest that far from idealizing either animals or people, or superimposing moral meaning onto them, Francis was only too aware of their fallibility. Francis was not sentimental about animals, seeing them as creatures with a particular function in the structure of the natural world. Consequently, following the gospel instruction to 'eat what is set before you' (Luke 10.8), Francis allowed his fraternity to eat meat, as he himself did. This was unusual among religious communities at the time.

Insects and other small creatures

> What shall I say about the other lesser creatures? In the winter he had honey or the best wine put out for the bees so that they would not perish from the cold. He used to extol the artistry of their work and their remarkable ingenuity, giving glory to the Lord. With such an outpouring, he often used up an entire day or more in praise of them and other creatures … this man, full of the spirit of God never stopped glorifying, praising, and blessing the Creator and Ruler of all things in all the elements and creatures. (I.250)

Offering praise and thanksgiving to God were fundamental to Francis in everything. As a result, these themes recur frequently in all writing about him, often inspired by nature or animals.

However, Francis did not always get things right, which is immensely reassuring for those of us who err frequently. Bee-keepers have watched honey bees drink a drop of alcohol and then fly off apparently slightly dazed. Bees, like you and me, cannot drink much wine without being affected, so it is probably best for them not to be encouraged to drink any at all. Honey, on the other hand, keeps a colony of bees going in a long hard winter and any extra from the bee-keeper will be helpful. So Francis was half right!

A further recurring theme in the record of Francis' relationship with creation is seen in another bee story. Francis had spent 40 days in a small cell on a mountain. Some time later, visitors found that the clay cup he had used was full of honeycomb and bees, 'symbolizing the sweetness of the contemplation which the holy one of God drank in at that place' (II.356). These are likely to have been bumblebees, which unlike honey bees create a nest and live as a small colony which could easily fit into a drinking cup. In this example, Francis' biographer Thomas of Celano was using bumblebees to record again the saint's devotion to prayer, in response to Jesus' example of praying alone on a mountain. The spiritual energy, depth of prayer, overcoming of temptations, and holiness implicit in a 40-day solitary retreat were assumed to leave so sweet a record at this isolated

cell that bees made it their home. Thomas gave such significance to this little tale that he allocated to it its own chapter.

A final bee story has a very different feel:

> There was a brother among them who prayed little, did
> not work, and did not want to go for alms because he was
> ashamed; but he would eat heartily. Giving the matter some
> thought, blessed Francis knew through the Holy Spirit that
> the man was carnal. He therefore told him: 'Go on your way,
> Brother Fly, because you want to feed on the labour of your
> brothers, but wish to be idle in the work of God, like Brother
> Drone that does not want to gather or work, yet eats the work
> and gain of the good bees.' So he went his way. (II.201–2)

Here we find Francis using the animal world to provide a
characteristic for an idle brother, taking a fly and a drone (a
male bee) for comparison. Francis clearly wished to imply that
brothers fly and drone share in being idle. While we can see
his point immediately, in a technical sense this comparison
does not stand up to any detailed examination. Whatever we
think about flies, they are not idle, and they form an incredibly
significant part of nature's food chain, providing calories for
many species. Similarly, while worker bees industriously collect pollen and nectar essential for a colony's nutrition, there
would be no bees at all if drone bees were truly idle. Once
again, like giving wine to honey bees, Francis, who had limited
formal education, is perhaps a man of his time in not fully
understanding life cycles or characteristics for some members
of the animal kingdom.

A last insect story is of a cricket that lived near Francis' cell.
Francis said: '"Sing, my sister cricket, and with joyful song
praise the Lord your Creator!" The cricket ... began to chirp,
and did not stop singing until the man of God, mixing his
own songs with its praise, told it to return to its usual place'
(II.357). When instructed, the cricket sang with Francis making
all those present 'so happy with her praises'. After eight days
he gave her permission to leave because he was worried that he
and his companions would 'vainly boast' about sister cricket.

Francis' regard for the cricket's singing led to both joyfulness in fraternal appreciation of creatures and creation, and
deeper love and praise for God the Creator. We can also see
in this story Francis' constant concern with non-possessiveness, which underpins his attitude to poverty. Although sister
cricket had been encouraging praise and giving great happiness, she was sent away so that any temptation to 'vainglory'
or pride, potentially aroused by her obedience, was removed
(his amazed companions had 'admired how obedient and tame
she was to him' (II.218)). Additionally, it is likely that Francis'
'seeing' of the tiny cricket contributed to his understanding of
God as Creator of an intricate and interrelated universe. Today
we might describe this within the context of the rich living
matrix that sustains our life on this planet: plankton, oxygen,
soil, plants, pollinating insects and so on.

Similar themes are apparent in Francis' relationship to that
humblest of creatures, the earthworm:

> Even for worms he had a warm love, since he had read this
> text about the Saviour: I am a worm and not a man. That is
> why he used to pick them up from the road and put them in a
> safe place so that they would not be crushed by the footsteps
> of passers by. (I.250)

> He was drawn with the same compassion ... to vile and lowly
> creatures ... even worms ... He diligently noted the virtue
> of these and all other creatures, and whatever he was able
> to judge as admirable, delightful or of value in any of them,
> he referred totally to the glory of the Maker of all things
> ... he contemplated the power, wisdom and goodness of the
> Creator of all in all things. (I.400)

Here we see Francis compassionately valuing worms, small
ones within God's creation, noted as lowliest and most vile. In
them he saw something of himself, partly, his biographer tells
us, because of Psalm 22.6 ('I am a worm and no man'), itself
based on Isaiah 41.14.

This attitude, of each person or creature as a very small but delighted in, honoured, intricate and necessary component of the Creator's handiwork, points once again towards an understanding of the interrelatedness of all that has been made. It emphasizes the inherent value of every component within the cosmos, from smallest microbe to largest mammal. Additionally, it helps us to see the foundation and origin of Francis' core value, humility, with its Latin root *humus* meaning earth.

Humble earthworms can be said to link dry land and vegetation (day three in the six days of creation: Genesis 1.1–24). Without worms recycling vegetation into earth, earth would not be able to feed creatures (day six). Worms themselves start the predatory food chain as they are the staple diet of so many birds. Interrelatedness and valuing are integral to the very earthy and pragmatic twelfth-century attitude to nature's cycle of life and death, shared by Francis (for examples see II.229 and II.311). When people died, their bodies became food for worms and so fed soil and earth from which all creation emerged.

Consideration of worms raises two aspects of Francis' relationship with creation. First, although Francis rarely mentioned worms in his writings he did note the common outlook at the time that those who died in sin without making penance would lose both body and soul because worms would eat their bodies (I.43, I.51). He used scriptural quotations to encourage his readers to leave sin behind and truly live observing Jesus Christ's way. As so often, an example from the natural world became spiritually symbolic for Francis.

Second, Francis wrote:

> Let us hold our bodies in scorn and contempt because, through our own fault, we are all wretched and corrupt, disgusting and worms, as the Lord says through the prophet: I am a worm and not a man, the scorn of men and the outcast of the people. (I.48)

Throughout his life, Francis was hard on his body, eating a very poor diet that sometimes included ashes, praying all night, going out in all weathers, rolling in snow, sleeping rough and so on. In the fraternity's early days he was equally hard on his companions. As time went on, he became more understanding of their frailties and inability to keep up with him. This can be seen in the story of a brother waking at night tormented by hunger because of excessive fasting. Francis, in compassion, gave him bread and they ate together (II.149, II.565). Elsewhere, he is recorded several times reproving friars who were too austere with themselves (II.102, II.259).

What are we to make of such a harsh attitude to his own body? As we have seen, Francis not only valued and loved all creation but also saw through it to God the Father and his incarnate son, Jesus Christ. Yet he writes these difficult words, quoting again from Psalm 22.6, instructing us in how we should relate to our bodies. It has been suggested that 'bodies' here refers to the personal 'I', the egotistical self (I.48). Read through such a lens, this text becomes Francis encouraging his readers to put aside all selfishness and self-centredness to focus on 'the commands and counsels of our Lord Jesus Christ' (I.48).

While this interpretation might seem reasonable to contemporary readers, we cannot escape from the historical reality of Francis' relationship with his body, which would actually have seemed quite usual for someone trying to live a holy life in the twelfth century. The Assisi Compilation contains a whole chapter (II.149–50) entitled 'Austere with himself, he was compassionate with others', in which Francis warns against excessive abstinence 'because the Lord desires mercy not sacrifice'. The same chapter records Francis' view of himself: 'I must be the model and example for all the brothers ... content with poor food and things, not fine ones.' This suggests that his awareness of needing to be an exemplary role model contributed to his excessive personal abstinence (II.599).

Mammals and fish

Lambs carried unique significance for Francis: 'Among all the different kinds of creatures, he loved lambs with a special fondness and spontaneous affection, since in Sacred Scripture the humility of our Lord Jesus Christ is frequently and rightly compared to the lamb' (I.248). This had interesting consequences:

> He came upon a shepherd in the fields pasturing a flock of goats. There was one little sheep walking humbly and grazing calmly among these many goats. When blessed Francis saw it, he stopped in his tracks, and touched with sorrow in his heart, he groaned loudly, and said to the brother accompanying him: 'Do you see that sheep walking so meekly among those goats? I tell you, in the same way our Lord Jesus Christ, meek and humble, walked among the Pharisees and chief priests. So I ask you, my son, in your love for Him to share my compassion for this little sheep. After we have paid for it, let us lead this little one from the midst of these goats.'
> (I.248–9)

On spotting a lamb among goats, Francis immediately once again saw 'an allegorical likeness to the Son of God' (I.248). However, this holy man, who was committed to poverty and did not carry money, immediately wanted to buy the lamb to free it from the goats' company. The story goes that a passing traveller paid for the lamb and it was given to the sisters at San Severino.

A further encounter was with two lambs:

> A man on his way to market ... was carrying over his shoulder two little lambs bound and ready for sale. When blessed Francis heard the bleating lambs, his innermost heart was touched ... showing his compassion. 'Why are you torturing my brother lambs,' he said to the man, 'binding and hanging them this way?' 'I am carrying them to market to sell them, since I need the money,' he replied. The holy man asked: 'What will happen to them?' 'Those who buy them will kill

them and eat them,' he responded. At that, the holy man said: 'No, this must not happen! Here, take my cloak as payment and give me the lambs.' The man readily gave him the little lambs and took the cloak since it was much more valuable. The cloak was one the holy man had borrowed from a friend on the same day to keep out the cold. The holy man of God, having taken the lambs, now was wondering what he should do with them. Asking for advice from the brother who was with him, he gave them back to that man, ordering him never to sell them or allow any harm to come to them, but instead to preserve, nourish, and guide them carefully. (I.249)

There is a tension here. Farmers make a countryside living by rearing and selling animals. In contrast, saintly Francis saw God in all creation, particularly lambs, and felt compassion for these two on their last journey. A somewhat other-worldly outcome ensued, reflecting these competing motivations. Having been paid for and saved from market, the lambs were handed back. Francis' holy, compassionate and God-centred vision must have appeared totally impractical to the shepherd, for whom, we may assume, lambs were a commodity necessary to pay bills and so on. A similar tension was noted earlier, when a large fish was caught and given to Francis: he promptly undid all the fisherman's time, hard work and hope of income by putting it straight back in the lake.

These stories demonstrate difficulties with aspiring to a life of poverty. In the first story, a charitable passer-by bailed out the brothers. In the second, we have no record of the reaction of the friend whose valuable cloak was borrowed only to be exchanged away. We also have no record of the fisherman's response on witnessing Francis releasing his hard-worked-for catch.

The tension in this meeting of worlds is significant for us reflecting on Francis' relationship with creation for several reasons. First, underpinning both these accounts is Francis' love for his neighbours (including lambs and fish), resulting in his compassionate action. He was motivated by a 'deep sense of concern not only toward other humans in need but also toward mute, brute animals' (I.248). Second, those who radically follow the way of Jesus Christ may have insights that others, caught up in their everyday world of family and work and paying bills, cannot see. Third, those who have money will always have power in ordering the world's workings. Fourth, challenging the status quo can be a drastic method to engage two worlds with each other (e.g. Jesus overthrowing temple money-changers' tables). Similarly, truly following the Christian way may lead to actions that appear ludicrous, extreme or other-worldly to some people. Last, those who act radically or challenge the status quo may need funding to sustain their action/challenge, perhaps coming from supporters, friends and well-wishers.

A final episode concerning lambs takes us back to arguably a harsher side of Francis' relationship with animals, confirming that any idealized or rose-tinted view of his relationship with the animal world is misplaced. He was staying at a monastery when a lamb was born overnight. Sadly it was soon bitten and killed by a sow. In the morning, the sow's responsibility for the lamb's death was clear. Francis was very affected by this incident, which reminded him of the death of 'that other Lamb' on the cross. He publicly cursed the vicious sow, which became ill and died three days later, its body not fit for consumption (II.321). Here we see again Francis' constant allegorical vision of nature: the lamb became symbolic of Christ, the Lamb of God, and the sow became evil incarnate, deserving punishment and social uselessness by being inedible (like the fig tree cursed by Jesus).

Another example of the non-idealized side to Francis' relationship with animals occurred at San Damiano during his final illness, when he was near his life's end:

There were many mice in the house and in the little cell made of mats where he was lying ... They were running around him, and even over him, and would not let him sleep. They even disturbed him greatly at the time of prayer. They bothered him not only at night, but also during the day, even climbing up on his table when he was eating, so much so that his companions, and he himself, considered it a temptation of the devil, which it was. (II.185)

Francis and his brothers appear to have accepted this plague of mice. They clearly regarded them as a major nuisance, but Francis neither stilled them (as with the birds) nor killed them (as with the sow). Instead, any temptation to exercise power or be distracted from prayer appears, from this account, to have been resisted. These descriptions of irritating mice and a sow's death suggest that Francis' relationship with animals in God's creation was not idyllic and cannot be neatly described or boxed off. Like the animal world itself, this relationship could perhaps best be described as varied and at times messy.

Less obviously messy are accounts about foxes and the wolf at Gubbio:

We who were with him often heard him repeat the saying of the holy Gospel: Foxes have dens and the birds of the air have nests; but the Son of Man has nowhere to lay his head.

And he would say: 'When the Lord stayed in solitude where he prayed and fasted for forty days and forty nights, He did not have a cell or a house built there, but He sheltered under the rocks of the mountain.' And so, after His example, he did not want to have a house or cell in this world, nor did he have one built for him. Moreover, if he ever happened to say to the brothers: 'Prepare this cell this way,' he would refuse afterwards to stay in it, because of that saying of the holy Gospel: 'Do not be concerned.'

Shortly before his death, he wanted it written in his Testament that all the cells and houses of the brothers ought to be built only of mud and wood, the better to safeguard poverty and humility. (II.159)

As noted earlier, biblical phrases were central to Francis' thinking and relating. The references to foxes (Matt. 8.20; Luke 9.58) and 'do not be concerned about what to eat or wear' (Matt. 6.31, 34; Luke 12.22) are typical of his radical and direct logic. This influenced his relationship to creation, leading him towards poverty, preferring the provisional and impermanent in his attitude to accommodation. Such a radical approach to following biblical directions, no 'ifs' or 'buts', is yet another challenge to those of us for whom security of place, employment or finance are priorities. It certainly challenged his fraternity during his lifetime: he once started throwing roof tiles off a recently constructed friary as he thought it too opulent (II.157)!

The story of Gubbio's wolf, which emerged from oral traditions (Vauchez, 2012, p. 275), is well known:

> A particularly fierce wolf was devouring some of the townspeople's livestock at Gubbio, and it had also been killing some of the people. Attempts to kill it had failed, and citizens lived in fear. Francis visited and, hearing the problem, decided to speak with the wolf. They met and he blessed the wolf with the Sign of the Cross. Recognizing that Francis had come in peace and was not a threat, the wolf went to Francis and curled up next to him. Francis proposed that if the wolf stopped menacing the townspeople, they would provide for him. The wolf extended his paw, signalling agreement, while the townspeople watched from afar. Francis and the wolf walked back into town, and wolf and townspeople both accepted the agreement. The wolf never troubled Gubbio again, and the citizens kept their bargain by feeding him. He lived among them for two more years as an honoured guest. (Adapted from III.482 and III.601)

Over many centuries, saints have been noted to befriend aggressive animals, particularly wolves, thus protecting local populations. Records have been traced back as far as St Macarius and the desert fathers (Armstrong, 1973, pp. 200–17). This account fits the recurring Franciscan theme of being fraternal to all animals, wild or domestic. In his writings, Francis instructed his readers to be 'subject and submissive ... not only to people but to every beast and wild animal as well' (I.165). The consequence, we can infer, is not domination of or aggression towards animals and creation but celebrating brotherhood, being alongside and sharing.

This belief in fundamental fraternity and relationship is perhaps what gave Francis confidence to carry on travelling when warned of dangerous wolves on the track ahead (II.807). Words from Isaiah may also have offered him biblical inspiration: 'The wolf and the lamb shall feed together' (Isa. 65.25). Such an attitude to relationship addresses another issue, that of exclusion. Violence between wolf, townspeople and livestock was overcome by welcome, dialogue, inclusion and a peaceful attitude. Exclusion in any form promotes intolerance and hardening of hearts. The Franciscan way is one of peaceful relating rather than fearfully creating an enemy.

This in turn leads us to reconciliation. It has been suggested that rather than being a physical wolf, Gubbio's terrorizer was in fact a local outlaw or brigand (Armstrong, 1973, pp. 200–4). While this interpretation seems unlikely, it emphasizes that Francis consistently advocated peace and frequently worked for reconciliation between people. Examples include visiting the Sultan in Egypt and, late in his life, reconciling the bishop and mayor in Assisi. Gubbio's wolf demonstrates Francis extending reconciliation beyond people to all creation.

This did not mean that Francis in any way idealized animals. He did not mention them much in his writings. He was happy to eat them, particularly fish. As we saw earlier (the sow, the robin), he could be as firm with them as he was with errant members of his fraternity (Brother Fly). This suggests an overall relationship with all creation that was pragmatic while also being fraternal, respectful and reconciliatory.

Before leaving animals, there is a note in *The Earlier Rule* in which Francis is clear about his fraternity, pets and horses:

> I command all my brothers, both cleric and lay, that when they go through the world or dwell in places they in no way keep any animal either with them, in the care of another, or in any other way. Let it not be lawful for them to ride horseback unless they are compelled by sickness or a great need. (I.73)

Brothers could enjoy interacting with animals in their lives but were not to possess them, presumably because their care could interfere with prayer, preaching, work, begging and other activities of the early fraternity. Additionally, keeping pets and riding horses were seen as signs of affluence at that time, which Francis associated with pride. As a young man, he is recorded as riding out on a horse during his expeditions as a knight and when he met and kissed the leper. Once he was established in a mendicant way of life he always walked, unless he was unwell, in which case he sometimes reluctantly rode on a donkey.

The first biography of Francis closes with a long account of the nativity enacted at Greccio. Christ's incarnation was always at the core of what Francis did. His faith was Christ-centred and hence he particularly valued the nativity. It is because of this episode in 1223 that Francis is often regarded as the founder of all subsequent nativity celebrations.

For blessed Francis held the Nativity of the Lord in greater reverence than any other of the Lord's solemnities. For although the Lord may have accomplished our salvation in his other solemnities, nevertheless, once He was born to us, as blessed Francis would say, it was certain that we would be saved. On that day he wanted every Christian to rejoice in the Lord and, for love of Him who gave Himself to us, wished everyone to be cheerfully generous not only to the poor but also to the animals and birds. (II.130)

Fifteen days before Christmas, Francis asked one of his friends to prepare a real live Christmas scene with ox, ass and infant in a hay-filled manger. All the brothers and many local people attended on Christmas Eve with candles and torches. The night was lit up, the forest echoed with the joyful crowd's cries, Francis preached, mass was celebrated and Greccio was made a new Bethlehem. Afterwards, everyone went home with joy. (adapted from I.255–6)

Inanimate creation

Francis' compassion for and love of all creation within God's love can frequently be seen in his respect for inanimate things: he had a fraternal relationship with them, and they often moved him to prayer, praise and preaching. The chief example of Francis' relationship with non-animate creation is provided by the Canticle of the Creatures, discussed in Chapter 3. Other examples include water, light, rocks and flowers:

> When he washed his hands, he chose a place where the water would not be trampled underfoot after the washing. (II.192)

> He spares lanterns, lamps, and candles unwilling to use his hand to put out their brightness which is a sign of the eternal light. (II.353)

> He walked reverently over rocks, out of respect for Him who is called the Rock. When he came to the verse 'You have set me high upon the rock,' [Ps. 27.5] in order to express it more respectfully, he would say: 'You have set me high under the feet of the Rock.' (II.354)

> How great do you think was the delight the beauty of flowers brought to his soul whenever he saw their lovely form and noticed their sweet fragrance? He would immediately turn his gaze to the beauty of that flower, brilliant in springtime, sprouting from the root of Jesse ... Whenever he found an abundance of flowers, he used to preach to them and invite them to praise the Lord, just as if they were endowed with reason. Fields and vineyards, rocks and woods, and all the beauties of the field, flowing springs and blooming gardens, earth and fire, air and wind: all these he urged to love of God and to willing service. (I.251)

The historical records also provide clear evidence of Francis' attention to and care for what we would now call a whole ecosystem:

When the brothers are cutting wood he forbids them to cut down the whole tree, so that it might have hope of sprouting again. (II.354)

He used to tell the brother who took care of the garden not to cultivate all the ground in the garden for vegetables, but to leave a piece of ground that would produce wild plants that in their season would produce 'Brother Flowers'. Moreover, he used to tell the brother gardener that he should make a beautiful flower bed in some part of the garden, planting and cultivating every variety of fragrant plants and those producing beautiful flowers. Thus, in their time they would invite all who saw the beautiful flowers to praise God. (II.192)

He commands the gardener to leave the edges of the garden undisturbed, so that in their season the green of herbs and the beauty of flowers may proclaim the beautiful Father of all. (II.354)

Brother woodsmen or gardeners were to leave enough tree so that it might regrow, perhaps as when hedges are layered today. Brother gardener was not to cultivate all garden ground for vegetables. Instead he was to leave untouched corners and edges for herbs and wild plants, which we might call weeds, so that their beauty when flowering could declare God's praise. These passages, which hint at instructions in Leviticus (e.g. Lev. 19.9), could even be interpreted to imply that Francis was giving directions about land being left fallow and crop rotation, but this is perhaps an embellishment too far.

In this chapter we have considered stories concerning Francis and creation, both animate and inanimate. Many themes and issues have arisen which will be summarized and discussed further in Chapter 4. Before turning to that task, we first explore Francis' relationship with creation using as our guide the Canticle of the Creatures, also known as the Canticle of Brother Sun. Despite its name, a significant proportion of this canticle relates to inanimate creation.

Questions for reflection

- Which stories of Francis and creation do you find helpful or unhelpful, and why?
- What do these stories tell you about your own relationship with all creation?
- How do you manage times when you have to be pragmatic in that relationship?

Further reading

Edward Armstrong, 1973, *Saint Francis: Nature Mystic – The Derivation and Significance of the Nature Stories in the Franciscan Legend*, Berkeley, CA: University of California Press.

Adrian House, 2000, *Francis of Assisi*, London: Pimlico.

Roger Sorrell, 1988, *St Francis of Assisi and Nature: Tradition and Innovation in Western Christian Attitudes Toward the Environment*, Oxford: Oxford University Press.

3

Francis and the Canticle
of the Creatures

¹ Most High, all-powerful, good Lord,
Yours are the praises, the glory, and the honour, and all blessing,
² To You alone, Most High, do they belong,
and no human is worthy to mention Your name.
³ Praised be You, my Lord, with all Your creatures,
especially Sir Brother Sun,
Who is the day and through whom You give us light.
⁴ And he is beautiful and radiant with great splendour;
and bears a likeness of You, Most High One.
⁵ Praised be You, my Lord, through Sister Moon and the stars,
in heaven You formed them clear and precious and beautiful.
⁶ Praised be You, my Lord, through Brother Wind,
and through the air, cloudy and serene, and every kind of weather,
through whom You give sustenance to Your creatures.
⁷ Praised be You, my Lord, through Sister Water,
who is very useful and humble and precious and chaste.
⁸ Praised be You, my Lord, through Brother Fire,
through whom You light the night,
and he is beautiful and playful and robust and strong.
⁹ Praised be You, my Lord, through our Sister Mother Earth,
who sustains and governs us,
and who produces various fruit with coloured flowers and herbs.
¹⁰ Praised be You, my Lord, through those who give pardon for Your love,

and bear infirmity and tribulation.
[11] Blessed are those who endure in peace
for by You, Most High, shall they be crowned.
[12] Praised be You, my Lord, through our Sister Bodily Death,
from whom no one living can escape.
[13] Woe to those who die in mortal sin.
Blessed are those whom death will find in Your most holy
will,
for the second death shall do them no harm.
[14] Praise and bless my Lord and give Him thanks
and serve Him with great humility. (I.113–14)

The church of San Damiano, just outside Assisi, is one of the places in which St Francis began his journey from partying youth to saint. If you stand with your back to this little church's west end, two statues can be seen. The first, nearest to you and on your right, is of St Clare standing and holding up the sacrament as a reminder of when she protected her sisters from marauding Saracens intent on violence. A few metres further west, on your left, you come across Francis, sitting cross-legged on the ground, looking out over the Vale of Spoleto.

This small statue shows Francis composing the Canticle of the Creatures at San Damiano while staying in the care of Clare and her sisters. The view from the sculpture is out over a vast valley surrounded by distant hills. This was Francis' world: he rarely travelled far from Assisi during his life; his furthest regular destination was the mountain retreat of La Verna (about 100 kilometres from Assisi).

The date was 1225, near the end of his life, some six to nine months after receiving the stigmata, when he was suffering greatly from several illnesses including malaria and malnutrition. How much he would actually have seen, had he sat where the statue sits, is open to question. He had impaired vision due to eye disease, probably trachoma or contagious conjunctivitis granulosa. The *Assisi Compilation* records that at that time he had to stay in darkness as he 'was unable to bear the light of the sun during the day or the light of a fire at night' (II.185).

Nevertheless, in our imaginations we can picture Francis

looking out on this view of his world and being inspired to give thanks and praise for all creation. And what a praise it turned out to be. One of the few texts to be written – or more accurately dictated – by Francis, it is in his local Umbrian dialect rather than the formal Latin of more educated people, which he never fully learned. Described as 'Francis' most celebrated masterpiece' (Hammond, 2004, p. 137), 'the first great poem in the Italian vernacular' (Thompson, 2012, p. 123), it 'reveals more than any other writing or legend Francis' feelings about nature' (Vauchez, 2012, p. 277), 'the end result and surely the supreme expression of a whole life' (Leclerc, 1977, p. x). It is especially significant in our consideration of Francis and creation because almost all the evidence we have explored so far has been writing about Francis, rather than his own words.

Chronology and structure

One night at San Damiano, 'Francis was reflecting on all the troubles he was enduring' when 'he was told in spirit':

> 'Brother, be glad and rejoice.' ... The next morning on rising, he said to his companions ... 'I must rejoice greatly in my illnesses and troubles and be consoled in the Lord, giving thanks always to God the Father, to His only Son, our Lord Jesus Christ, and to the Holy Spirit for such a great grace and blessing. In His mercy He has given me, His unworthy little servant still living in the flesh, the promise of His kingdom.
> 'Therefore ... I want to write a new Praise of the Lord for his creatures.' ... Sitting down, he began to meditate and then said: 'Most High, all-powerful, good Lord.' He composed a melody for these words and taught it to his companions so they could repeat it. (II.185–6)

There were three stages to the composition of the Canticle. Verses 1 to 9 were written in April or May 1225 when Francis' health was poor and his living conditions were extremely difficult. Mice and other vermin infested the hut at San Damiano where he was staying. After the instruction to 'be glad and rejoice', he was inspired to write these verses. They form the main part of the poem and are particularly concerned with praising God for creation.

Next, in June or July 1225 at the bishop's house in Assisi, where Francis was confined to his bed, came verses 10 and 11. The focus of these two verses is forgiveness. The final two verses, dealing with death (12 and 13), were dictated to Brother Pacifico at the end of September or the very beginning of October 1226, during the last few days of his life. It is likely that verse 14 was a refrain, used after each verse of the entire Canticle. Francis is reported to have set it to music but sadly the tune has never been found.

Francis wrote the Canticle of the Creatures in a similar way to many of his other prayers of praise to God, in using doxologies. A doxology is a prayer of praise (from the Greek *doxologia* meaning 'words of glory') such as the familiar 'Glory to the Father and to the Son ...' said after psalms and canticles, or the 'Gloria in excelsis'. Verse 14 ('Praise and bless my Lord') is a repeated doxology occurring eight times. This provides the prayer's central and essentially simple structure.

The Canticle's structure can also be seen in its overall descending movement, beginning with the Most High, then the divine symbolism of Sir Brother Sun and the complementary darkness lit by Sister Moon and the stars, then through Wind, Water and Fire down to Mother Earth. Into this created wholeness the final four stanzas integrate enduring and inevitable decline, infirmity and death alongside hope of a divine destiny.

Sources

When writing anything, the primary source for Francis was always his extensive biblical knowledge, especially Scripture involved in the fraternity's regular liturgy. For example, we know from Francis' own surviving breviary, dated 1223, that Psalm 148, the Laudate Dominum, was sung daily at Lauds at daybreak. He also sang The Song of Three Young Men in the furnace (Dan. 3) on Sundays at Lauds: verses 55–65 became known as the Benedicite. Psalm 148 and The Song of Three Young Men are key influences of and sources for the Canticle of the Creatures, along with Francis' earlier prayers, especially The Praises to be Said at all Hours (I.161), the Exhortation to the Praise of God (I.138) and A Salutation of the Virtues (I.164) (Moloney, 2013, pp. 56–64; Sorrell, 1988, pp. 98–114).

There are numerous other biblical links throughout the Canticle. Examples include, in verse 3, 'Praised be You, my Lord, with all Your creatures', which alludes to Genesis and the Psalms. 'Sister Moon and the stars, in heaven You formed them' from verse 5 can be linked directly to Genesis 1.14. The second death, in verse 13, refers to eternal death sourced from Revelation. Whatever we learn from Francis' Canticle, its authority comes from these firm biblical foundations.

Troubadour poems and lyrics have been suggested as another source (Moloney, 2013, p. 54). Francis loved these and could recite them: he is recorded as singing praises in French in a forest (I.194, II.142). Rather than direct sources, it is more likely that they were simply joyful influences on both music and words. During the composition of the Canticle, Francis created a melody and wanted to send for Brother Pacifico, a singer, to lead other brothers preaching and praising God using the Canticle (II.186). We might call them God's troubadours.

Jesus Christ was such a central focus for Francis throughout his life that the lack of any specifically Christian vocabulary in this text ('mortal sin' excepted, verse 13) is surprising. When he wrote the Canticle, it had been over a year since Francis had experienced God's grandeur on La Verna as he received the stigmata. It seems reasonable to suggest that this experience of mystical union became a source of inspiration for the Canticle and also shifted Francis' focus from the Son towards all members of the Trinity, particularly God the Father. This supreme illumination of the soul might account for the overwhelming praise of God the Father throughout the Canticle: almost every verse starts 'Praised be You, my Lord'.

A complementary suggestion is that in the Canticle Francis is giving thanks for his own new birth within a new creation

(Vauchez, 2012, p. 280). We can hear the voice of Christ, particularly in the words 'pardon', 'love' and 'peace', along with the allusion to the Beatitudes: 'Blessed are those who endure in peace' (verses 10 and 11).

Praise and thanksgiving

The Canticle is both a poem and a prayer of thanksgiving to the Creator. Praise is given not to creatures themselves but to God who made them beautiful and useful. The usual translation of the Canticle, given above, has the Italian preposition *per* as meaning 'through': 'Praised be You, my Lord, through Brother Wind, Sister Water', and so on. There is, however, great discussion among scholars about this translation. *Per* can also mean 'for' ('Praised be You, my Lord, for Brother Wind ...'). This is seen as the most likely alternative. Other possibilities are *per* meaning 'by' ('Praised be You, my Lord, by Brother Wind ...': the elements themselves give praise to God) or 'by means of', in which humans praise God together with creatures (Hammond, 2004, pp. 142–5; Sorrell, 1988, pp. 115–24; Thompson, 2012, pp. 269–70).

While this point might seem a little theoretical, the possible meanings allow us to interpret Francis' words in a variety of helpful ways: as giving thanks and praise to the Creator *for* the world, *together with* the world and *through* or *by* the world. So the Canticle can also be read as an instruction to humankind to praise God and his creatures/creation: 'be praised, my Lord and all your creation (Sister Moon, the stars, etc.), by humankind' and 'be praised, my Lord, by humankind for and because of all your creation'. In addition, it can be read as an instruction to all creation to praise God: 'be praised, my Lord, by all your creation including humankind'. The latter – creation seen as active in praise – may feel odd to us but would have been a quite normal interpretation in medieval times.

Both these options (the Canticle as an instruction either to creation or to humankind) would have been present in thirteenth-century thought. Either way, the Canticle of the

Creatures is Francis' ultimate prayer of praise, written with the intention of encouraging all creation and creatures, including humankind, to praise their Lord.

By directing his brothers to go into the world preaching, praising and singing his Canticle using the local Italian dialect, Francis intended this praise to be spread far and wide to instruct and help people: 'Therefore for His praise, for our consolation and for the edification of our neighbour, I want to write a new Praise of the Lord' (II.186). Such edification or instruction might be received in several ways. The most obvious and probably intended response remains simply praise and gratitude for all creation. A sense of intimate joy underpins and explodes from this prayer of praise to God. For example:

> Be praised, my Lord, with all your creatures,
> Especially Sir Brother Sun ...
> How handsome he is, how radiant, with great splendour! ...
>
> Be praised, my Lord, for Brother Fire, ...
> How handsome he is, how happy, how powerful and strong!
> (translation by Sorrell, 1988, p. 101)

Other possible responses include valuing creation as symbolic (the sun as signifying God); as beautiful (Brother Fire); as useful (the sun gives light, the earth feeds people); as ecological (valuing the interconnectedness of creation as an ecosystem); as fraternal (the family of all creation: brother, sister, mother); or simply for its inherent God-given worth (irrespective of any value or usefulness to humans) (Doyle, 1997, pp. 38–54; Sorrell, 1988, pp. 123–4).

Fraternity, interdependence and the Canticle

The text praises God through celestial bodies (Sun, Moon, Stars) and elements (Air, Water, Fire and Earth). Striking omissions are living creatures, including humans, and Jesus Christ, whose name does not appear at all. Despite his love for them, we can imagine Francis leaving creatures out of his composition, given the conditions in the cell in which he was writing. Day and night, numerous mice were so tormenting him that he was seeing them as temptations and works of the devil (II.185). Although he must have found this very trying, he had previously written that creatures merited more than humans because they serve and obey their Creator and did not crucify him (I.131). Within the whole of creation overall, Francis saw animals' role and witness in giving praise and worship as no different from that of humans: a universal fraternity.

This vision of a universal fraternity, seeing all creation in respectful relationship as brother, sister or mother, was fundamental to Francis. It was soundly and biblically rooted in his Christian faith. He wrote:

> O how happy and blessed are these men and women ... children of the heavenly Father Whose works they do (Matt. 5.45), and they are spouses, brothers, and mothers of our Lord Jesus Christ (Matt. 12.50). We are spouses when the faithful soul is joined by the Holy Spirit to our Lord Jesus Christ. We are brothers to Him when we do the will of the Father who is in heaven (Matt. 12.50). We are mothers when we carry Him in our heart and body. (I.41)

We have already seen how this fraternity extended to creatures: 'he calls all animals by a fraternal name' (II.354), including 'My brother birds' (I.234). All this, according to St Bonaventure, emerged from prayer:

> From a reflection on the primary source of all things, filled with even more abundant piety, he would call creatures, no matter how small, by the name of 'brother' or 'sister', because he knew they shared with him the same beginning. (II.590)

Francis had renounced his own family as a young man, at the Bishop of Assisi's residence (I.193). Over the years, this absence may have contributed to his vision and welcome of all creation as within God's family. So in his poem, earth becomes both reverentially and productively mother, and affectionately sister; Sir Brother Sun, beautiful and signifying Christ, is given deep respect linked to fraternal love; 'our Sister Bodily Death' is also named as a natural and welcome relative in this extended family. Within this sisterhood and brotherhood we can see gender complementarity and equality, feminine no less significant than masculine in God's scheme:

> Sun, fire, wind and weather are masculine because the qualities associated with them are power and robustness; the moon, water and the earth are praised for their gentleness and generosity, the moon for her clarity, water for her cleanliness, earth for her fecundity. (Armstrong, 1973, p. 231)

Such gender complementarity is not always obvious in the early records of incidents concerning the saint (see, for example, II.323). Any bias is most likely to come from biographers rather than from Francis himself, who clearly frequently met women and for whom St Clare and Lady Jacopa were highly significant friends (Armstrong, 1973, pp. 230–5).

Underlying this vision of fraternity is Francis' assumption of a wider family involving interdependence between creation, humanity and God. While creation can serve people and humans can depend on creation's help, creatures can also depend on humans for their well-being (such as lambs saved on their way to market, fish released). Francis had a view of humans at times being subservient to creation (I.165) and certainly tried to live this out: for example, out of respect for Brother Fire, he urged his brothers to allow their cell on La Verna to burn when it became alight (they put it out, he went off into the forest!) (II.191); and despite a feeling of panic, he obediently accepted cautery to his eyes by 'beautiful and useful ... courteous ... gentle' Brother Fire (II.354–5).

The 'courteous' nature of relationship with Brother Fire hints at the knightly ideals of chivalry such as bravery, hospitality, generosity, almsgiving, honesty and loyalty that were prevalent at the time and influenced Francis significantly as a young man before his turnaround. Courtesy to all people, including one's social inferiors, was inherent in the spirit and personality of a chivalrous person. This, it has been suggested, permeates the whole Canticle and puts Francis, other people and all creatures on the same level (Moloney, 2013, pp. 113–21).

As in any realistic view of family life, Francis' vision of fraternity is not all rose-tinted. The *Assisi Compilation* records his initial motivation to write the Canticle as follows:

> I want to write a new *Praise of the Lord* for his creatures, which we use every day, and without which we cannot live. Through them the human race greatly offends the Creator, and every day we are ungrateful for such great graces, because we do not praise, as we should, our Creator and the Giver of all good. (II.186)

Although the Canticle is Francis' great prayer of praise and thanksgiving, this comment emphasizes his very pragmatic understanding of the relationship of humans to the rest of creation. In the previous chapter, we saw examples of this down-to-earth approach (the robin, the sow, worms eating dead humans, friars eating meat). This note in the *Assisi Compilation*, concerning humanity's many failings and selfishness in relation to the rest of creation, suggests that during Francis' lifetime imbalances and difficulties were already present. This leads Doyle to propose that the Canticle is, in part, a protest against humanity's misuse of creatures (Doyle, 1997, p. 67).

There are many examples demonstrating Francis' view that 'all creatures, separate in functions, worth, desires, and beauty, are bound together in a harmonious interdependence ensured and presided over by the just and benevolent eye of God' (Sorrell, 1988, p. 133). Nevertheless, the Canticle's simple language conceals a complex vision of reciprocity and interrelationships. Creatures are equal brothers and sisters to each other, performing their divinely allotted tasks. As beings aided by other creatures, humans honour creation's service and beauty by giving God thanks for it. This thanks and praise form the basis of the process of reconciliation that is needed when difficulties arise, such as we see towards the poem's end between Assisi's mayor and bishop.

The notion of interdependence running throughout the Canticle also points us towards the concept in contemporary biology of ecosystems. While being unheard of as a concept in the thirteenth century, it would undoubtedly have been experienced in everyday living, especially perhaps in subsistence farming which consumed many poor people's lives in central Italy at that time. If all creation, including us, is interlinked and interrelated, then respect and care are needed. For Sister Mother Earth to sustain and produce, she herself needs nurturing: manure needs to be spread before good growth will occur; pruning may be necessary; overplanting or removing too much (e.g. timber, fish) need to be balanced in the interests of long-term sustainability and productivity.

Humans and the Canticle

For the first time in a written prayer since The Prayer before the Crucifix 20 years earlier, Francis used the first person possessive 'My Lord' throughout the Canticle. With this change of grammar, and by also using the fraternal titles Brother and Sister throughout, Francis united himself, all creation, and all who read or pray these words (including you and me) in God's family under 'the universal fatherhood of God' (Leclerc, 1977, p. 11). Despite this, as we have already noted, humans are hardly mentioned in the Canticle of the Creatures, appearing directly only in verse 2, where they are noted as unworthy to name God.

In a sense it is us, human readers, who narrate the poem while gazing on the world's beauty and contemplating God in wonder: 'Humanity is creation become conscious of itself. The human voice therefore speaks on behalf of all that is created' (Doyle, 1997, p. 70). The latter applies when we pray any prayer, not just the Canticle of Creation.

Although the Canticle is a carefully written poem expressing

Francis' experience and feelings, it was undoubtedly meant to be read or sung aloud as a joyful proclamation and celebration in praise and thanksgiving for God's goodness and forgiveness. Its rhythms and repetitions, and the use of Umbrian rather than Latin, would have made it accessible to all listeners, not just to educated people. In a way, it was written as a tool for evangelism for lay people. Unusually for his time, Francis believed that ordinary lay people, not just priests and religious, could live a full Christian life leading to God's salvation. Hence his initiation of the Third Order.

The Canticle also hints at the possibility that through God's benevolent creation humanity is provided with all its needs. Sun, water, weather and earth all contribute to produce enough crops for the population's requirements. Francis is perhaps saying that there is no need for the trading and exploiting by the merchant society that he so dramatically renounced. A social model involving full sharing with all creation of the gifts of that creation would allow peaceful coexistence among all creation.

The last five verses of the Canticle relate directly to humans without naming them. Verses 10 and 11 aimed to create forgiveness and reconciliation between the all too human figures of mayor (podesta) and bishop in Assisi. They had fallen out and were in open conflict: the bishop had excommunicated the mayor and the mayor had made it a crime for people to have any legal dealings with the bishop. Francis recruited two of his brothers to sing the revised Canticle publicly in front of both men, urging reconciliation and peace: this appeal was successful. In these two verses, Francis can also be seen to universalize his own experience of forgiveness and illness, making it clear that God's love and forgiveness are available to all.

Verses 12 and 13 befriend death 'from whom no one living can escape'. Written when Francis was 'racked with sickness' but 'praised God with great fervour of spirit and joy', they were intended for 'consolation of his own soul and that of others' (II.121). The final refrain (verse 14) is simply an instruction to human readers or singers: 'Praise and bless my Lord and give Him thanks and serve Him with great humility.'

Verses 6 to 9 emphasize that creation has been made for human beings. Elements within creation sustain, produce and are useful 'to us'. Through the Canticle, humanity is invited to share sabbath rest and enjoyment, participating in God's joy in creation: 'God saw everything that he had made, and indeed, it was very good' (Gen. 1.31). This Franciscan celebration of all creation was counter-cultural, coming against a backdrop of religious belief at the time that was largely world-denying. This was particularly true for a group known as Cathars. Considered in Francis' time to be heretics, they believed that the spiritual world had been created by a beneficent divine power, and so was good. Contrastingly, they viewed the material world in which humans live out their earthly lives as inherently evil, having been created by an evil God (Moloney, 2013, p. 108; Sorrell, 1988, p. 77). In turn, this contrasts with today's profoundly secular consumerist Western society which so often pushes any belief in a spiritual world or life to one side. The result is that any contemporary Franciscan approach to, or celebration of, creation may be seen as once again counter-cultural.

The Canticle as interior journey

The Canticle is the unconscious, symbolic expression of an interior journey – the journey Francis was making all his life and in which an affective union with the humblest created things was joined with a spiritual ascent to the heights (Leclerc, 1977, p. 132).

Reading the Canticle as an interior journey offers a different way to see Francis' relationship with creation. In searching creation for the sacred and spiritual, we symbolize our inner searching for our own interior sacred, spiritual and divine. This section offers a few pointers but is in no way comprehensive.

The sun has carried symbolic meaning for millennia. The early Christians gathered on the Sun's day, on which God put darkness to flight. They turned in prayer towards the rising sun as a symbol of Christ's rising from the dead. Francis used to say: 'At dawn, when the sun rises, everyone should praise God, who created it, because through it the eyes are lighted by day' (II.186).

The sun also carries an inner meaning. St Teresa of Avila noted that the 'divine sun' was abiding 'in the midst' or 'at the centre' of her soul, referring both to her deeper self and to God (Teresa of Avila, 1995, p. 10). For Jung, the sun was the image of interior psychic fullness, found in the depths of one's being (Jung, 1956, p. 122). So Francis' celebration of Sir Brother Sun can be seen as honouring both the physical sun that warmed, illumined and energized all creation, and the divine interior sun giving life in our souls. St Paul put it like this: 'God who said, "Let light shine out of darkness", who has shone in our hearts to give us the light of the knowledge of the glory of God' (2 Cor. 4.6).

In contrast to the permanence of the sun, the moon fluctuates and changes through its cycle, a symbol of hope as it disappears for three days and then returns fresh and new. It reflects the sun's light just as we are called to reflect God's light and love in our lives. Inevitably, our ability to offer such reflection will also fluctuate and change over time.

The spiritual significance of night lies in part in its association with souls wrestling with life's depths and mystery. Often seen as a feminine maternal symbol, the moon illuminates the darkness of night, again offering hope. Unlike his praise of Brother Sun's action in giving light and day, Francis in his Canticle praises Sister Moon and the stars as clear, precious and beautiful. These are values simply of being rather than of useful action. They symbolically point towards the importance of integrating deeply within each of us passivity and activity, feminine and masculine, dark and light.

Sister Water is also a feminine symbol, indispensable, part of the new life of baptism. Francis' adjectives – useful, humble, precious and chaste – again suggest integration of feminine and masculine. For masculine Francis, this feminine appears not shadowy or repelling but open and worthy of praise. Just as Brother Wind and every kind of weather contribute to Sister Water, so the Spirit blows on the waters of life giving sustenance. This hints at the possibility of in-dwelling, spiritual experience mediated through the elements of creation.

Fire is one of the great symbols of humanity's life and energy, both life-giving and destroying. Francis loved fire: 'He was moved with such piety and love for it that he did not want to blow out a candle, a lamp, or a fire' (II.191). He was unwilling 'to put out their brightness which is a sign of the eternal light' (II.353). Each fire was symbolically a window into the blazing light and life of God. Oil lamps and candles still continually burn in many churches to symbolize sacred presence.

In Sister Mother Earth, Francis links sustaining and governing Mother Earth with sisterly affection. He also writes that she creates beauty through flowers suggesting joy throughout creation. Implicit in this is mother as source of new life, which emerges from the womb's darkness into creation's light and plenitude. In the Scriptures, death is part of life: seed dies and returns to earth before new life can occur. So Francis asked to die naked on bare earth, returning to and reconciled with the creation from which he was made prior to his spiritual new life in Christ.

The initial version of the Canticle finished with Sister Mother Earth. The remaining verses address pardon, peace and death and can be said to have a common theme of peaceful reconciliation. All creation is offered God's gift of unlimited forgiveness, extending even into the deepest, blackest parts of our inner selves, however unforgivable or unworthy we feel. We in turn are called to forgive and so be peacefully reconciled with ourselves, other people and all creation. This includes accepting, welcoming and praising death's central role within creation, within life and within each of us.

Francis' constant greeting of 'May the Lord give you peace' demonstrates his fundamental belief in friendship, mercy, respect, hope, reconciliation and equality between all components of God's creation, human, non-human and inanimate. It opposes the dualism between humans and the natural world so prevalent in modern Western society. For Francis, all creatures have their source in the same creative love and this common origin is the basis of all relationship or, as he would say, brotherhood: 'the Most High himself is present at the roots of reality and flourishes in all things' (Leclerc, 1977, p. 185). So the kingdom of God is present at the interior core of our most ordinary everydayness. To live and celebrate this joyfully, healing and reconciling the divide between humanity and creation, human and divine, is central to the Franciscan charism.

The Canticle helps us to see Francis' interdependent relationship with his fellow creatures clearly. 'Praised be You, my Lord, with all Your creatures', he wrote. In these words we hear his tenderness and love towards the world around him. Francis' contribution through his Canticle is to help us see creation as our brother and sister – in need of great love and care as well as providing for us. Against a contemporary backdrop of religious belief that was largely world-denying, this celebration of the world and all creation in reverence and compassion was new and stood out. His approach still stands out today.

Questions for reflection

- How do praise and joy feature in your life, and might this need to change?
- What part does inanimate creation play in your prayer and your action?
- Which symbols have meaning for your interior journey?

Further reading

Jacques Dalarun, 2016, *The Canticle of Brother Sun: Francis of Assisi Reconciled*, St Bonaventure University, NY: Franciscan Institute Publications.

Eloi Leclerc, 1977, *The Canticle of Creatures: Symbols of Union*, Chicago, IL: Franciscan Herald Press.

Brian Moloney, 2013, *Francis of Assisi and His Canticle of Brother Sun Reassessed*, New York: Palgrave Macmillan.

4

Francis, Spirituality and Creation

The church of Santa Maria Maggiore, cathedral of Assisi until the eleventh century, is tucked away off a quiet, small square, semi-detached to the house and offices of the Bishop of Assisi. It was in the Renunciation Room of the bishop's residence that Francis dramatically stripped off his clothes. He handed them back to his father, Pietro di Bernardone, declaring that from now on his only father would be his father in heaven (I.193, II.251). In Giotto's painting of this scene in the Upper Church of the Basilica of St Francis in Assisi, Bishop Guido is wrapping his own cloak round Francis.

North of the church, a small garden contains a statue of Francis wrapped only in some sort of cloth and running with one arm outstretched, pointing to the heavens. There is a sense of immediacy in this figure, of hurrying to important work while treading lightly on our planet. Leaving family commerce behind, supported by his church, and with minimal possessions, the statue captures Francis beginning a new relationship with God the Creator and with all God's creation.

In this chapter we will explore themes that have emerged so far in Francis' relationship with creation. We will also consider some features of his life and way of living in order to tease out key components of what we today might call his spirituality of creation. This will then form the basis of the rest of our book, in which we discuss how followers of Francis have lived and developed this spirituality over the centuries, and are responding to its challenges in contemporary times.

Incarnation and creation

Some Christians may wonder, why study the life of a medieval friar when there is plenty of teaching to guide us in the Scriptures, and when we have the inspiration of God's Holy Spirit speaking in our hearts? To this a Franciscan might say that we attempt to follow Francis' example because we believe that he himself walked so closely in the footprints of Jesus his Lord. Francis was an evangelical Christian in the full meaning of that term – the gospel of Jesus Christ was his life's guiding principle. He was deeply devoted to Jesus, and sought to follow him in all things, always singing God the Father's praises and invoking the Holy Spirit's aid.

To this end, Francis was steeped in the Holy Scriptures, reading and reciting them day and night, quoting them liberally in all his writings. Like many of his day, he would have memorized large portions of the Bible, particularly the Psalms. In addition to the standard eight services of prayer and praise each day (known as the Daily Office), he put together in his *Office of the Passion* collections of Psalms to remind him of the events of the last few days in Jesus' life. Some of the offices and letters that he wrote are almost entirely collages of Scripture with little or no original material from Francis. He had an excellent memory (I.202) and so this writing most likely came from within him rather than from hours spent poring over sources to assemble suitable texts.

The reason for Francis' devotion to Scripture, and particularly the Gospels, was their revelation of God in Jesus Christ:

Let us therefore hold onto the words, the life, the teaching and the Holy Gospel of Him Who humbled Himself to beg His Father for us and to make His name known saying: Father, glorify your name and glorify Your Son that Your Son may glorify You. (I.81)

Francis' faith was focused on Jesus – it was Christocentric. 'Whoever sees me, sees my Father,' Francis wrote, quoting John 14.6–9 (I.128). In looking at Jesus he found the image of God, and in looking at his fellow creatures he found the image of Jesus: 'O human being ... the Lord God ... created and formed you to the image of His beloved Son according to the body and to His likeness according to the Spirit' (I.131).

Additionally, as we noted earlier, when looking at creation, Francis saw God's image. All creatures, including human beings, and all creation were seen as coming from the same divine source, the same loving Father. So all aspects of creation bore God the creator's image, were God's gift, and revealed God.

Through incarnation, the one through whom all things were created came to be a creature. This was crucial for Francis and remains a central foundation for Franciscan spirituality: all things are fellow creatures with God's incarnate Son and are therefore brothers and sisters. They can be humans or animals but they can also be flowers, rocks, sun, moon and stars, or the elements of earth, water, fire and air.

In relating deeply to the person of Jesus, Francis learned to love, value and offer praise with all aspects of creation. The whole of creation became the place of encounter with God: all creation was holy, nothing was trivial or worthless, and all things pointed beyond themselves to their Creator. Consequently, worms were taken off paths, a live nativity was enacted at Greccio, and flowers received preaching to encourage them to praise God their Creator. St Bonaventure described this as seeing God's footprints impressed in all creation (II.596–7) and it remains a core component of Franciscan spirituality.

Eucharist and creation

Francis' Christ-centred focus, inspired by the incarnation, resulted in turn on his emphasis on the importance of the Eucharist: another characteristic of Franciscan spirituality linking to his approach to creation. 'Appearing humbly,' wrote Francis, 'each day He comes down from the Father ... in the hands of a priest ... In this way the Lord is always with His faithful' (I.129):

O sublime humility!
O humble sublimity!
The Lord of the universe,
God and the Son of God,
so humbles Himself
that for our salvation
He hides Himself
under an ordinary piece of bread! (I.118)

Francis saw Jesus Christ, God's Son incarnate, choosing at every eucharistic celebration to be humbly among people in the form of bread: bread, so ordinary and everyday, a staple food known as God's gift in creation for millennia, but also God's hiding place. Infinity is contained in the simple and finite, remembered at every eucharistic celebration: the Son of God, in-mattered and so in-human-ed in the 'little form' of bread (Short, 1999, p. 43). This is God's humility, gift hiding within creation in the ordinary and the unremarkable.

This insight was a foundation of Francis' understanding of and relationship with all creation, and it underpins a Franciscan spirituality of creation. In Francis' eyes, the divine Word voluntarily chose poverty, humility and simplicity as a form of life. In his writings, Francis urged his readers and followers to choose to follow the divine Word's example by living in poverty, humility and simplicity in their own lives, and so draw close to God. Choosing to live in this way will inevitably profoundly affect how each person relates to all aspects of creation.

Francis' reverence for eucharistic bread led him to also honour church buildings as precious places because they represented and housed the God of love, present through prayer and sacrament (I.124–5). Perhaps because of this, he sometimes spent the night alone praying in abandoned churches (I.244). Similarly, whenever the brothers saw a church, they would turn towards it, prostrate themselves on the ground, bow inwardly and outwardly, and offer the prayer of adoration taught them by Francis: 'We adore you, O Christ, in all your churches ...' (I.222). Once again, through reverencing churches as precious places, Francis saw God's presence in creation.

Poverty and creation

Francis' adoption of poverty was a response to Jesus' choice to give up divine status, become incarnate, and take on lowliness as a poor man dying on a cross. Near the end of his life, Francis wrote that the Lord revealed that he 'should live according to the pattern of the Holy Gospel' (I.125). This led him to embrace poverty, which included living 'without anything of [his] own' (I.100).

In some of his teachings to his brothers known as *The Admonitions* (I.128–37), Francis described what this meant in practice. He noted, from the Beatitudes, that they were to be 'the poor in spirit for theirs is the kingdom of heaven' (Matt. 5.3). They were to leave all that they possessed and not seek positions of authority. Those who were educated or studied Scripture were not to use their knowledge to accumulate riches. 'The Most High Himself ... says and does every good thing' (I.132): all good things, which included all creation, belonged to God, and to take anything to oneself was considered envy and blasphemy.

For Francis, this was not poverty as penance, or in any way being set against material things, but was considered a response to God's generosity. Possessions would get in the way of appreciating God's great gift. For example, Francis noted that if the brothers owned a monastery or hermitage, weapons would be needed to guard it (I.471). By living and praying as poor mendicants, Francis and his fraternity were dependent on God as the original source of every thing, giver of all being, and so could draw close to Christ by sharing poor people's lives. He noted in the *Later Rule*:

> As pilgrims and strangers in this world, serving the Lord in poverty ... they should not be ashamed because, for our sakes, our Lord made Himself poor in this world. This is that sublime height of most exalted poverty which has made you, my most beloved brothers, heirs and kings of the Kingdom of Heaven, poor in temporal things but exalted in virtue. Let this be your portion which leads into the land of the living. (I.103)

In adopting poverty as a key component of his fraternity's way of life, Francis defined their relationship with God and with all God's creation. This consisted of non-possessiveness, letting go and lowliness. It had numerous consequences, some of which will become apparent later, and it underpins any Franciscan spirituality of creation.

Francis was keen that the brothers should work, as noted in the story of Brother Fly: they only begged if they could not work for some reason. When they worked for others, they would receive payment in kind such as bread and fruit, as Francis rejected all contact with money itself. They lived in 'poor little houses built of mud and wood' (II.161) with small cells for prayer so that their visible humility and holy poverty would preach to visitors.

Praise and creation

Praise, joy and thanksgiving, often inspired by creation, emerge from the stories and evidence that we have been reviewing as key attributes of Francis' life. For example, the Canticle of the Creatures ends 'Praise and bless my Lord and give Him thanks': Francis' original intention was that the Canticle should be set to music and sung, and that this final verse should be a refrain sung after every verse. Another example is the story of Francis and the singing cricket, which led Thomas of Celano to note that 'Blessed Francis found so much joy in creatures because of love of the Creator' (II.218). Commenting on the same story, St Bonaventure added that the cricket's song 'aroused the Lord's servant to the divine praises' (II.593).

Early records concerning Francis are clear that praise, joy, adoration and thankfulness were central to his daily living and were a model to those around him. There are numerous examples in his writings of directions to praise, thank and adore God (I.76, I.88, I.134), and of his own prayers of praise, thanksgiving and adoration (I.78, I.109, I.113–14, I.138, I.161–2):

All-powerful, most holy, most high, supreme God: all good, supreme good, totally good, You Who alone are good, may we give you all praise, all glory, all thanks, all honour, all blessing, and all good. So be it! So be it! Amen. (I.162)

Any attempt to understand and live out Francis' view of creation must include these as core components. This is because for Francis the intricacies and interrelatedness of nature and all created things pointed beyond themselves towards the infinite loving goodness and generosity of God their Creator. All reality expressed God's goodness, so all reality was called to praise, adoration and thanksgiving (I.49). Fully expressing this in his life embedded Francis in a long biblical and ecclesiastical tradition.

The Te Deum starts: 'We praise you, O God, we acclaim you as the Lord; all creation worships you, the Father everlasting' (*Common Worship*, p. 802). The Benedicite, a Song of Creation taken from the biblical Song of the Three, begins, 'Bless the Lord all you works of the Lord' (Dan. 3.35–65). It then names many of these works, urging them to bless and praise the Lord for ever. These include sun, moon, stars, rain, winds, light, darkness, mountains, hills, all that grows in the ground, seas and rivers, birds, beasts and people. Psalm 148 similarly directs all creation to praise the Lord:

Praise the Lord from the earth,
you sea monsters and all deeps ...
Mountains and all hills,
fruit trees and all cedars!
Wild animals and all cattle,
creeping things and flying birds!
(Ps. 148.7–10)

Preaching and creation

Preaching was central to the mission of Francis and his fraternity. At one stage in his life, he felt he faced a clear choice between being an evangelist and living a hermitage life of prayer, contemplation and solitude. He sought advice from Sister Clare and Brother Sylvester, who both responded that he should preach. On receiving these replies, which Francis took as 'God's will', 'he rose at once, girded himself and without the slightest delay took to the roads ... to carry out the divine command ... he ran along so swiftly as if the hand of God were upon him, giving him new strength from heaven' (II.622–4).

Earlier, as we explored Francis' relationship with creation, we discussed his sermon to the birds (I.234). In that episode, we saw Francis learning that his mission was not simply to humans: birds, and hence all creation, needed to hear the word of God. From then on, Francis preached to all creatures so that they might recognize their individual worth, praise and thank God, and 'participate in the world of apostolic harmony Francis hoped to restore among humankind' (Sorrell, 1988, p. 67). He instructed his brothers to preach, sing the praises of the Lord as minstrels, 'move people's hearts and lift them up to spiritual joy', and then call their listeners to turn to God in penance (II.186). In putting all this into practice, Francis was fully participating in traditional Christian mission as directed by Jesus: 'Go into all the world and proclaim the good news to the whole creation' (Mark 16.15). Perhaps this is the true meaning of Francis' running statue in the church garden of Santa Maria Maggiore in Assisi.

Relationship and creation

Incarnation, eucharist, poverty, praise, prayer: each of these factors shaped, and in turn were shaped by, Francis' overall relationship with all aspects of creation. In the paragraphs that follow, we explore this relationship further.

First, Francis' relationship with creation was not static, it evolved as he matured in his Christian journey. For example, in the sermon to the birds, when Francis approached the birds they did not take flight as birds usually do. So Francis asked them to listen to God's word and preached to them. The text suggests that if the birds had flown away no preaching would have occurred: it was the choice of the birds to stay that allowed Francis to respond. Later, we are told, he reflected and accused 'himself of negligence because he had not preached to them before. From that day on, he carefully exhorted all birds, all animals, all reptiles, and also insensible creatures, to praise and love the Creator' (I.234). Another example of Francis' relationship to creation changing over time was his attitude to physical hardships endured by his brothers. He became less hard on them and more understanding of their frailties.

Second, Francis came to have a sibling or fraternal relationship with creation, in all of which he saw God, and God's love and generosity. We have seen something of this in the previous sections in which we noted Francis' prayerful vision of a universal fraternity within which all creation was integrated as brother or sister, sharing inherent worth, with gender complementarity and equality, all underpinned by respect and courtesy.

From the evidence that we have reviewed, it is hard to disagree that 'in Francis' view, all creatures, separate in functions, worth, desires and beauty, are bound together in harmonious interdependence ensured and presided over by the just and benevolent eye of God ... [with] emphasis on mutual service, respect and affection' (Sorrell, 1988, p. 133). Francis' vision of autonomy and equality with interdependence and reciprocity between humans and all aspects of creation was new in his time. He lived it out practically in routinely blessing all creation (humans, animals, inanimate creation) on departing from them and in his emphasis on reconciliation, respect, courtesy, care and nurturing. Examples of such Franciscan reconciliation were both between nature and humans and between humans and humans (Gubbio's wolf, Egypt's Sultan, Assisi's mayor and bishop).

Third, it is significant that Francis could be very pragmatic concerning creation and its relationship to humans, perhaps coming from his vision of all creation as a family under God. Within families, loving relationships coexist with necessary restraints such as disciplining children. He emphasized death as a central part of life, noting worms consuming people's bodies. Unlike other religious orders at the time, he allowed his fraternity to eat animals, both meat and fish (I.66).

Francis could also be extremely unpragmatic towards creation. He released animals caught for food. He became caught up in prayer through natural events such as the crossed branches of trees or roadside hedges reminding him of Christ's cross (I.222). Spontaneous joy towards all creation 'because of love of the Creator' (II.218) would arise in him. His overwhelming love of God found throughout creation is perhaps seen best in the Canticle of the Creatures. The divine light symbolized in Brother Fire is also in each of us, allowing us to join with all creation in sharing the new life of Mother Earth and so to integrate passive and active, male and female, dark and light. God's gift of unlimited forgiveness points us towards equality between every element of creation, including Sister Death, embracing peaceful and hopeful reconciliation.

Fourth, Francis was very clear that his relationship with creation had limits. It was not going to be one of power or ownership or possession, which might lead to pride or obstruct prayer. Examples include instructing his brothers to live as pilgrims and strangers (I.103); enjoying interacting with animals but not keeping any themselves (I.73); giving sister cricket permission to leave so that there could be no chance of a brother developing pride or possessiveness for her (II.357); refusing to continue using a cell that a brother described to him as 'your little cell', suggesting ownership (II.159). This attitude contributed to his choice of living in poverty and minority, and challenges many contemporary attitudes towards, for example, pets and possessions.

The story of the fish given to Francis led Thomas of Celano to record that 'the glorious father Francis was worthy of the great honour before God of having the obedience of creatures' (I.236). Many writings about Francis similarly note that animals obeyed him, though it is most likely that these are medieval writers' hagiographical embellishments: having power over animals was considered a mark of holiness. There is no evidence of Francis himself seeking to have any power over creation: he embraced humility and powerlessness, calling his fraternity Lesser for this reason.

In summary, Francis saw himself as an integral component of creation in which all things revealed to him God's presence. His relationship with creation evolved as his Christian journey developed. It was based on respectful interdependence and equality, and necessitated forgiveness and peaceful reconciliation when necessary, both between people and between humanity and creation. It could be very pragmatic, but at times quite the reverse, and did not involve power or possession. It stands against the dualism between humans and the natural world so prevalent in today's Western society.

Francis, spirituality and creation

Perhaps the key Franciscan theme of all that we have reviewed in these pages so far is that of choosing to restore just and right relationships between humans and creation. In Francis' time, everything was thought to have been created through God and God's Word. So Francis saw all creation as interdependent and interrelated and journeying towards God, giving each component intrinsic dignity and worth. Humans were viewed as unique in their ability to love freely and make choices. If, as Francis believed, the kingdom of God is now and we are called to participate in it through our lives and how we live, then restoring worth, equality and justice for all peoples and all things is a central priority. This approach to the natural world was much more positive than was usual in Francis' time: it remains profoundly counter-cultural to today's consumerist, individualistic and largely secular Western lifestyle.

Francis' example points us towards constantly choosing non-possessive peaceful relationship and reconciliation between humanity, creation and God in everything we do. Additionally, it encourages us routinely to see God and God's loving gifts throughout creation, and so to live in joy, praise and thankfulness. These are key Franciscan themes.

How we might achieve all this is not straightforward but it arises in everything that we have discussed concerning Francis and creation. His example challenges us to value every component of creation (worms, flowers, wolves, rocks and so on) as much as we value humans, because all are family, equal and interrelated in God's creation. Viewed this way, it is a fundamental injustice to possess excessively and enrich oneself because this deprives others. It is also an injustice not to work for reconciliation in situations where right or peaceful relationships have broken down:

> The life and legacy of Francis remains a forceful reminder that the role of God's children is not only to be humble caretakers or stewards of creation, but indeed to be courageous liberators of their brothers and sisters in the mutuality of compassionate concern that the Creator intended from the beginning and desires at the end. (T. J. Johnson in Robson, 2012, p. 157)

Although to modern eyes sometimes both radical (e.g. stripping off at the bishop's residence) and impractical (e.g. buying sheep then giving them back), Francis' example can also be pragmatic (e.g. allowing brothers to eat fish and meat). It can point, as we have seen, to more modern biological, ecological and agricultural ideas such as ecosystems, planting diversity, conservation and land management.

The Canticle of the Creatures offers a view of creation based on a relationship of equals, with God as focus of all that is made. If all created things are linked in brotherhood and interrelatedness under God, then Francis prophetically points each of us towards a down-to-earth experience of God who has made an unchangeable decision to be incarnate. This is not a spirituality that calls us away from the world but rather invites us to closer engagement with creation. By attending to worldly creation, we attend to and meet God.

This central prophetic Franciscan insight is crucial because it challenges any spirituality that is not rooted in ordinary, mundane, down-to-earth, 'dirty feet', worldly life (Short, 1999, p. 128). For Francis, God's kingdom is already here and now, for you and for me, through participation in it. As a result, Francis and his followers are mendicant friars not monks, encountering God in the everyday world rather than leaving the world to find God. This is a creation spirituality emphasizing God revealed in Christ, in human form, enfleshed, 'in-mattered', in our history, and in our present (Short, 1999, pp. 128–9). Its inspiration is firmly rooted in remembering and praising God and God's generosity seen throughout God's wonder-full creation.

Along with the Canticle, Francis' writing that perhaps expresses this most fully and sums up his approach to creation is The Praises to be Said at All the Hours:

Let us bless the Father and the Son with the Holy Spirit:
And let us praise and glorify Him forever.

Bless the Lord, all you works of the Lord.
And let us praise and glorify Him forever.

Sing praise to our God, all you His servants
and you who fear God, the small and the great.
And let us praise and glorify Him forever.

Let heaven and earth praise Him Who is glorious.
And let us praise and glorify Him forever.

Every creature in heaven, on earth and under the earth;
and in the sea and those which are in it.
And let us praise and glorify Him forever. (I.161)

Questions for reflection

- If you were following the example of Francis' approach to creation, what would come easily to you and what would you find difficult?
- What might you need to change in your life to live in the Franciscan way?
- How might you express reconciliation, interrelatedness and minority in your everyday living?

Further reading

Brother Ramon, 1994, *Franciscan Spirituality: Following St Francis Today*, London: SPCK.

David Torkington, 2011, *Wisdom from Franciscan Italy: The Primacy of Love*, Ropley: O-Books.

Rowan Clare Williams, 2003, *A Condition of Complete Simplicity: Franciscan Wisdom for Today's World*, Norwich: Canterbury Press.

Franciscans and Creation

NICHOLAS ALAN WORSSAM

5

Living in Paradise

So far in this book we have been looking at the stories of St Francis and his relationship with creation. He was clearly remembered as someone with a finely tuned sense of both the suffering and the joy of others, humans and animals alike. Often he would be filled with pity for animals being caught or taken to market; and he rejoiced with what he saw as the praises of God being offered by the whole of creation, both animate and inanimate. He was deeply moved by the poverty and suffering of those around him, and as experienced by his Lord Jesus Christ; and he wanted as much as he could to live a simple life so that he would not be separated from those in need. Above all, he called all things brother or sister, so that, reconciled with all things, he might share with them in the kingdom of God. That reconciliation knew no bounds, reaching out to all in conflict, to his brothers and sisters in community, the wider Church and those of other faiths, and even to his sisters Mother Earth and Sister Death.

Now we come to explore further how the Order and spiritual tradition named after Francis developed over the subsequent years. This means seeking the wisdom of St Clare of Assisi, one of the first to join Francis in his new adventure. Then there were the friars educated at the universities of Paris and Oxford, such as Bonaventure of Bagnoregio and John Duns Scotus, who became increasingly influential in guiding the Order as to how best to respond to the needs of the Church. Others in the developing Franciscan tradition became known as the 'spirituals', people such as Angela of Foligno and Jacopone da Todi, who wrote towards the end of the thirteenth century about their rich religious experiences.

Francis himself was a saint, but he was not a born adminis-
trator. He rejoiced in his brothers and sisters living the religious
life in community, but he did not find it easy to organize them
into a structure that would endure for centuries to come.
Already within his own lifetime there were thousands of Friars
Minor or Lesser Brothers joining this new movement sweeping
across Europe; many of them had never met Francis.

In the collection of stories about Francis put together by some
of his closest confreres and known as *The Assisi Compilation*
there is an account of how Francis resigned from leadership in
the community he had founded:

> Blessed Francis wanted to be humble among his brothers. To
> preserve greater humility, a few years after his conversion he
> resigned the office of prelate before all the brothers during a
> chapter held at Saint Mary of the Portiuncula ... From that
> time on, until his death, he remained a subject, like one of
> the other brothers. He wished to be subject to the general
> minister and the provincial ministers, so that in whatever
> province he stayed or preached, he obeyed the minister of
> that province. (I.125)

Francis realized that the movement he had founded was beyond
what he could control, and that the church authorities were
now stepping in to help regulate this new community. Now
the dilemma was how to maintain the freshness of this new
vision of religious life while developing a structure that could
maintain stability and order: not an easy task in the face of
strongly held opinions that differed markedly about the correct
way forward. Towards the end of his life, Francis is reported to
have said: 'I have done what was mine to do; may Christ show
you what is yours' (II.386). In this section of our book we
will be discovering something of how Franciscans after Francis
responded to that challenge, and how they were inspired by
and adapted the tradition into which they entered, so as to help
us today know what we should do to honour the life of Francis
in our actions day by day.

Clare of Assisi and the song of creation

> She [the witness, Sister Angeluccia of Spoleto] also said when
> the most holy mother [Clare] used to send the serving sisters
> outside the monastery, she reminded them to praise God
> when they saw beautiful trees, flowers, and bushes; and like-
> wise always to praise Him for and in all things when they saw
> all peoples and creatures. (Armstrong, 2006, p. 187)

St Clare of Assisi (1193/4–1253), known as *la pianticella*, the
'little plant' of St Francis, was one of the first to heed the call
of Francis to a life of poverty and penance. A daughter of the
noble family of Favarone di Offreduccio, Clare lived a comfort-
able life in a large house at the centre of Assisi. But she longed
to follow Francis' example by devoting herself to a life of austerity and prayer. Escaping from the family home one night, she
ran to the woods outside Assisi's city walls, to the Church of
St Mary of the Angels, where she knew she would find Francis
and his small band of brothers. Perhaps this was a surprise to
Francis, but he nonetheless performed the rite of cutting her
hair to symbolize the renunciation of family life, and sent her to
a community of Benedictine nuns until it might become clearer
what her path should be. After some time of discernment, Clare
and the companions who were beginning to gather around her
settled at the abandoned church of San Damiano, rebuilt by
Francis himself, where they lived for the rest of their lives.

Clare was adamant that she and her sisters in religion should
live the simplest life possible, possessing no more than the
necessities of an enclosed life of prayer. The church authorities
wanted her to accept endowments, so as to make their monastery
financially secure, but Clare wanted no security other than that
offered by faith in God, that God would provide for them day
by day. She called it the 'privilege of poverty', and it was only
agreed to by the Pope at the last moment, as Clare lay dying
on her sickbed.

In the rule that Clare wrote for herself and her sisters, called
The Form of Life, which was the first religious rule for women
to be written by a woman, Clare writes:

Let the sisters not appropriate anything to themselves, neither a house nor a place nor anything at all; instead, as pilgrims and strangers in this world who serve the Lord in poverty and humility, let them confidently send for alms. Nor should they be ashamed, since the Lord made Himself poor in this world for us. (Armstrong, 2006, p. 119)

Clare wanted to be poor in material things but rich in virtue, always travelling light on the pilgrimage of this earthly life. This was her way of imitating the life of Christ, who lived as an itinerant preacher and healer of bodies and souls. Clare herself was blessed with the gift of healing, and people from Assisi would bring their loved ones to the monastery for her to make over them the sign of the cross. Far from turning her back on the world, Clare maintained a life of prayer that intimately connected her with the rest of the inhabitants of Assisi. Clare would send out sisters or brothers to ask the townsfolk for donations, thus maintaining her humility and acknowledging her dependence on others' generosity.

In her *Testament*, written at the end of her life, Clare explained her vision of religious life:

Let the sister who shall be in office [the abbess], however, as well as the other sisters, be attentive and farsighted that they do not acquire or receive more land about the place than strict necessity requires for a garden for raising vegetables. But if it becomes necessary for the integrity and privacy of the monastery to have more land beyond the limits of a garden, let no more be acquired or even accepted than strict necessity demands. This land should not be cultivated or planted but remain always fallow and uncultivated.

I admonish and exhort in the Lord Jesus Christ all my sisters, both those present and those to come, to strive always to imitate the way of holy simplicity, humility and poverty and also the integrity of our holy way of living. (Armstrong, 2006, pp. 63–4)

Clare presents a model of sustainable living, consuming no more than the absolute minimum for life, keeping the 'footprint' of the monastery no larger than was necessary for growing a few vegetables and maintaining the seclusion needed for a life of silence and prayer. And, as the first quotation above points out, she was, like her mentor Francis, well aware and appreciative of the beauties of nature.

I warm to her gentle encouragement to her sisters to 'praise God when they saw beautiful trees, flowers, and bushes'. Surrounding the monastery where I live in Worcestershire, we have a small parcel of land, just a couple of acres but enough to plant some fruit trees – apples, pears, plums and damsons – and to tend a few rows of gooseberry and blackcurrant bushes for harvest each June. And then within the monastery garden there are shrubs, some more, some less under control; and the perennial flowers that emerge where they will seem to flow around the herbaceous borders with a sense of direction all their own. As I write, the snowdrops are long gone, but the daffodils still stand tall and the primroses reveal themselves before being hidden again by taller daisies and anemones. Spring colours vividly return as the grape hyacinths rise like purple pyramids on stalks at the edges of gravel paths.

Appreciation of the natural world is an essential part of the life of prayer. Seeing the steady flow of the seasons year by year reminds us of the seasons of life and death that every living creature has to pass through. Hearing the singing of the birds tells of the social interactions that happen around us, the courtship and raising of families, the warnings about predators and the proclamations of 'private' territory not to be encroached upon by others. Last year a yellowhammer took up residence on the pinnacle of our roof. I enjoyed his song at first, but as summer drew on I would have preferred a blackbird to have claimed the podium instead. Trees have their own song, creaking and swaying in the wind, with storms rushing through the adjacent woods like tides of sound breaking over the monastery roof. Oak trees in particular have lives of patience to share, supporting whole communities of living beings, from the fungi connecting their roots to neighbouring trees, to the insects inhabiting the highest branches of the leafy canopy.

The Franciscan tradition was at heart an outdoor movement.

Today we sometimes hear of 'forest church', moving out of stone and brick churches into the natural cathedrals of wood and stream. But Francis of Assisi got there first! He spent much of his life out of doors, praying in the woods at night, living in simple huts with a small group of brothers, walking the roads and paths of his native Umbria. I think that is why he was able to instinctively build a rapport with animals. He knew their language, and they recognized the waves of compassion that flowed silently from him.

Brother Bonaventure: biographer and theologian

Francis died in the year 1226. Within two years he was canonized as a saint, and his fame spread far and wide as his followers, the Order of Lesser Brothers, travelled the roads of Europe and beyond, preaching peace and penance to all who would listen. Biographies, known in Latin as *legendae*, came to be written to preserve the memories of his deeds and words. One such writer was Brother Bonaventure (1217–74), a Minister General of the Order of Friars Minor, who described his understanding of the religious experience of Francis in his *Major Legend of Saint Francis*:

> Aroused by everything to divine love, Francis rejoiced in all the works of the Lord's hands and through their delightful display he rose into their life-giving reason and cause. In beautiful things he contuited Beauty itself and through the footprints impressed in things he followed his Beloved everywhere, out of them all making for himself a ladder through which he could climb up to lay hold of him who is utterly desirable. With an intensity of unheard devotion he savoured in each and every creature – as in so many rivulets – that fontal Goodness, and discerned an almost celestial choir in the chords of power and activity given to them by God, and like the prophet David, he sweetly encouraged them to praise the Lord. (II.596–7)

Bonaventure probably never met Francis, but he talked to Francis' closest companions and tried to summarize the most important aspects of the saint's life. His devotion to Francis is clear, but the words come from the scholastic style of the University of Paris at the close of the thirteenth century. Did Francis really 'contuit' Beauty in beautiful things? Would he even know what the word 'contuit' meant? (Something like 'have an intuition of' or 'discern'.) Was everything a ladder for Francis to climb up to God, or did he rather prefer to stay at the bottom of the ladder with the poor and outcast from society?

Bonaventure saw the image of the ladder of creation as an invitation to enter more deeply into the practice of contemplative prayer, polishing the mirror of the mind so as to perceive more clearly the reflections of the Divinity in creation. Thus following the footprints of God leads to savouring the rich variety of creation; and appreciation of the purity of nature as it springs forth from the abundant grace of God leads to participation in the 'almost celestial choir' of creation. These are very ecclesiastical images – reflecting the concern of Bonaventure, and Francis before him, to work for the well-being and unity of the Church. But the experience of God in the Church is rooted in the practice of personal prayer, another theme that was common to them both. So for Bonaventure the eyes of the spirit are opened by prayer to see God's attributes of power, wisdom and goodness shining forth in creation, reflecting the art of the creator; and the ears of the spirit are cleansed by the silence of contemplation, so as to hear more distinctly the song of creation. Bonaventure's image of Francis as a kind of cosmic choirmaster, 'sweetly encouraging' his singers as he conducts creation with a wave of his hands, connects us to an anecdote in *The Assisi Compilation*:

Sometimes he used to do this: a sweet melody of the spirit bubbling up inside him would become on the outside a French tune; the thread of a divine whisper which his ears heard secretly would break out in a French song. Other times – as I saw with my own eyes – he would pick up a stick from the ground and put it over his left arm, while holding a bent bow in his right hand, drawing it over the stick as if it were a viola, performing all the right movements, and in French would sing about God. (II.142)

Francis sang in French because that language reminded him of the troubadour songs of chivalry and romance that he learned while on business trips to France with his father, the cloth merchant Pietro di Bernadone. All his life Francis sang, and it was in song, in his Canticle of the Creatures, that he summed up the song of his life, as we saw in the previous section of this book.

Bonaventure and emanation

Bonaventure of Bagnoregio probably wouldn't have had time for secular songs, but he was arguably a poet of the spiritual life. Bonaventure was a highly trained theologian. He knew the value of words and the importance of logical reasoning. But that doesn't make his writings easy to understand! Sometimes reading a chapter of one of his books just leaves a modern reader with a headache and an urge to reach for the latest best-selling novel. But it is worth the effort to get inside his language, steeped as it is in the scholastic terms of his day, and to hear at least something of the message he still has for us. Bonaventure himself knew that language was not everything. Nonetheless, he loved to think, and to create intricately constructed theological works. In honour of the Holy Trinity, he would combine almost endless categorizations of spiritual teachings revolving around the number three. One such foundational text is found in his book *Collations on the Six Days*:

> The Word expresses the Father and the things He made, and principally leads us to union with the Father who brings all things together; and in this regard He is the Tree of Life, for by this means we return to the very fountain of life and are revived in it ... Such is the metaphysical Centre that leads us

back, and this is the sum total of our metaphysics: concerned
with emanation, exemplarity, and consummation, that is,
illumination through spiritual radiations and return to the
Supreme Being. (Bonaventure, 1970, pp. 9–10)

This passage brings out many of the key themes of Bonaventure's teaching to be explored in the pages of this book: how
the Father emanates the Son who through the creation leads
us back to the Father; and how the Word of God, the Second
Person of the Trinity, expresses God, shows us what God is
like and enables us to mirror his image. In this way Christ the
Word of God is the Centre of all things, showing us the Father,
and by illuminating our hearts and minds enabling us to return
to the Supreme Being. For Franciscans, Christ is our partner in
the dance of creation, who leads us back to the Tree of Life in
the garden of Paradise.

A clue to help us understand 'how things go forth from God'
(emanation) can be found in a classic of biblical wisdom literature, the Wisdom of Solomon, in a passage of great beauty:

Wisdom is more mobile than any motion; because of her
pureness she pervades and penetrates all things. For she is a
breath of the power of God, and a pure emanation of the glory
of the Almighty; therefore nothing defiled gains entrance into
her. For she is a reflection of eternal light, a spotless mirror
of the working of God, and an image of his goodness ... She
reaches mightily from one end of the earth to the other, and
she orders all things well. (Wisd. 7.24–26; 8.1)

Wisdom pervades all things, like the breath that God breathes
into all living beings, giving them life. Discovering wisdom in
all things is a delight, just as she delights in holy souls and
makes them friends of God. The author of the poem loves her
more than all things, and desires her as his bride.

Bonaventure meditated often on scriptural passages such as
this. In his book *The Tree of Life* he writes of Jesus as the
'Fountain-Ray of Light':

In this eternal kingdom, all good and perfect gifts come down in plenty and abundance from the Father of Lights through Jesus Christ, who is the superessential Ray and who, since he is one, can do all things, and renews all things while perduring (Wisd. 7.27) himself. For he is a pure effusion of the brightness of the power of the omnipotent God, and therefore nothing that is sullied can enter (Wisd. 7.25) into this Fountain-Ray of Light. (Bonaventure, 1978, pp. 170f.)

In *The Tree of Life*, Bonaventure has been considering the 'mystery' of the origin, passion and glorification of Jesus, just as many Christians do today when they say the Rosary and reflect prayerfully on the Joyful, Luminous, Sorrowful and Glorious Mysteries in the life of Jesus and his mother Mary. Just as Jesus momentarily revealed the radiant glory of his true nature on the Mount of the Transfiguration, so here Bonaventure describes Jesus as the Wisdom of God, the Fountain-Ray of Light holding all things in being. He then speaks directly to the reader and says:

You soul devoted to God, whoever you are, run with living desire to this Fountain of life and light and with the innermost power of your heart cry out to him: 'O inaccessible beauty of the most high God and the pure brightness of the eternal light, life vivifying all life, light illuming every light, and keeping in perpetual splendour a thousand times a thousand lights brilliantly shining before the throne of your Divinity since the primeval dawn! (Bonaventure, 1978, p. 171)

You can imagine Bonaventure gazing up at the night sky and marvelling at the enormity of the heavens, with all the stars shining brightly in the firmament above. And this was in the days before light pollution. Of course, this was also before the rise of modern astronomy, when people still thought of the earth as the centre of the universe; but that means that our sense of wonder today is surely multiplied a thousandfold, knowing something of the vast extent of the universe, let alone the multiple dimensions or parallel universes that astrophysicists tell us may possibly exist.

Bonaventure roots his theology always in the nature of God as a community of love, whom he often describes as a 'fountain' of love and joy, as Franciscan scholar Ilia Delio writes:

> Bonaventure's theology of creation takes as its starting point the Trinity of love. In the first book of his commentary on the Sentences, he writes that creation is like a river that flows from a spring, spreads throughout the land to purify and fructify it, and eventually flows back to its point of origin. This image not only speaks to us of Bonaventure's appreciation of the beauty of creation but it also indicates that he saw the deep intimate relationship between creation and the triune God. It is an image that imparts to creation vibrancy of life replete with the self-diffusive goodness of God. Creation flows from the fountain fullness, the spring of the creative and dynamic Trinity. (Delio, 2003, p. 22)

Bonaventure speaks in terms of the 'emanation' of creation from God, the emergence of all things by the divine Word. Creation was formed 'out of nothing' (Latin *creatio ex nihilo*). Bonaventure says in his *Breviloquium*: 'The entire fabric of the universe was brought into existence in time and out of nothingness, by one first Principle, single and supreme' (Bonaventure, 1963, p. 69). The doctrine of *creation ex nihilo* was designed to emphasize the sovereignty of God as the unchallenged 'first principle', bringing both matter and form into being by the free act of God's will. Delio explains further:

> Bonaventure describes creation as sharing in the mystery of the generation of the Word from the Father; it is a limited expression of the infinite and dynamic love between the Father and Son, emerging out of this relationship and exploding into a thousand forms in the universe. He uses the term 'emanation' (*emanatio*) to describe the birth of creation from the womb of the triune God of love ... Creation, he writes, is like a beautiful song that flows in the most excellent of harmonies but it is a song that God *freely* desires to sing into the vast spaces of the universe. That is, there is nothing

that compels God to chant the hymn of the universe. (Delio, 2001, p. 54)

The creation is not the result of God's spoken word only; rather, the universe is sung into being. This makes me think of the importance of hymnody and chant in Christian worship, and in so many religious traditions around the world. Certainly Francis loved to sing, whether in Latin, French or Italian, no doubt entertaining his brothers as they walked from town to town. By singing together, even if at times out of key or in varieties of rhythm, we are bringing something new into the world. To sing well there has to be a kind of letting go of each person's will to be the lead soloist of the choir, thus allowing the one heart and mind of the body of Christ to express itself through the one voice of the choir, the community itself becoming a multifaceted person made in God's image.

Certainly I find great consolation and encouragement in the singing of the psalms and canticles in our monastery chapel. Knowing that these words, in various translations, have been sung to similar melodies over thousands of years roots me in the family of faith that sustains me. Even Jesus of Nazareth sang the psalms (Mark 14.26); no doubt he chanted his prayers in solitary retreats into the Judean desert, or on the mountains in his nocturnal hours of prayer. Music emanates from God: it resonates within us, restructuring our physical being, and refreshing the overworked body and mind. Music both creates and recreates, calms and enlivens. So for Bonaventure, emanation signifies all creation as God's music and song.

John Duns Scotus and individuation

For Bonaventure, creation is quite literally a work of art. First God planned it all out in his mind, then put brush to paper without hesitation, like a Zen master drawing a perfect circle with a single sweep of his arm. Then, as the crown of his work, God revealed his designs in the life of Jesus, the exemplar or model of what it is to be both human and divine. So in the

Franciscan tradition, the incarnation is not a rescue mission designed to correct a defaced image, but the final masterpiece of the original plan, the magnum opus of one who has joyfully perfected his art.

This focus on the intricate link between creation and incarnation is a hallmark of the Franciscan intellectual tradition. One Franciscan friar who particularly emphasized this was the Scottish theologian Blessed John Duns Scotus (1265–1308). Coming from Midlothian, his name literally means 'John the Scot, from Duns'. In 1280 he made his vows as a Franciscan friar, and studied philosophy and theology at Cambridge and Oxford. At Paris he became Regent Master in Theology in 1305, following a run-in with the church authorities over his opposition to the election of Boniface VIII as pope. Scotus became known as the 'Subtle Doctor' because of the subtleties of the philosophy he taught. At the Reformation his name became a pejorative term, a 'dunce' becoming the word for someone who talked nonsense that no one else could understand. Nonetheless, Bonaventure and Scotus have been the two foundation pillars of Franciscan theology ever since the thirteenth century.

Delio explains Scotus' teaching on the incarnation, an essential part of the doctrine of exemplarism:

> Scotus maintains that God became human in Jesus out of love (rather than because of human sin) because God wanted to express God's self in a creature who would be a masterpiece and who would love God perfectly in return. This is Scotus's doctrine of the primacy of Christ ... the divine desire to become incarnate was part of the overall plan or order of intention. Scotus places the incarnation within the context of creation and not within the context of human sin. Christ, therefore is the masterpiece of love, the '*summum opus Dei*'. (Delio, 2003, p. 34)

Christ, the Son of God, of whom God says at his baptism, 'This is my Son, the Beloved, with whom I am well pleased' (Matt. 3.17), the one who dwells within us and within whom we dwell, is the prototype of all humanity, the model on which creation is based. But that doesn't mean that everything is the same. Rather, Scotus emphasizes the uniqueness of everyone and everything:

> His notion of individuation points to the idea that each particular being has its own intrinsic, unique and proper being. Scotus placed great emphasis on the inherent dignity of each and every thing that exists. We often perceive individual things through their accidental individual characteristics (e.g. size, shape, colour), but Scotus calls our attention to the very 'thisness' of each thing, the very being of the object that makes it itself and not something else (a 'not-that'); Scotus's notion of essential 'thisness' is known as the doctrine of *haecceitas* and relates to essential individuation. (Delio, 2003, p. 37)

Each and every thing in creation has value in its own right, and can only be known by direct acquaintance. Perhaps the best commentator on this teaching of Duns Scotus was the nineteenth-century Jesuit poet Gerard Manley Hopkins, in his use of the term 'inscape'. Many of Hopkins' poems seek to show this delightful awareness of the individuality of things, especially the sonnets:

> As kingfishers catch fire, dragonflies draw flame;
> As tumbled over rim in roundy wells
> Stones ring ...
> Each mortal thing does one thing and the same:
> Deals out that being indoors each one dwells;
> Selves – goes itself; myself it speaks and spells,
> Crying What I do is me: for that I came ...
> (Hopkins, 1970, p. 90)

Each thing does the same: 'Selves – goes itself'. Later in the poem this is explained as 'acts [as] Christ', but as Christ is the exemplar of all things, so the cry of each individual thing is its own particular way of sharing in the mystery that is Christ, through whom all things came to be (John 1.3). Everything is an infinitely precious, unique facet of the sparkling diamond of creation. Everything plays its own part, sings its own line in the score, harmonizes in the symphony of God's creative delight.

These two emphases of Scotus' teaching – God's creation of all things in love, and the absolute value of all things – are complemented by a reflection on the dignity of the creation, and how humanity is fully equipped to make appropriate moral choices. Franciscan theologian Mary Beth Ingham summarizes these three perspectives:

> In the first perspective, God is the artist and creation the work of art. Reflection upon the existence of the work in its contingency reveals something about its author. The second perspective focuses on each part of the whole to reveal its delicacy. Here, the insight is that each being plays an essential role in a much larger whole, a role that no other being can play. Attention to the particular reveals the profound dignity and sanctity of all that exists. The third perspective reveals how, in our own lives, we are naturally gifted with all we need to know this world and to appreciate its dignity. Each particular act of human knowing brings us closer to the God who created all that exists and who is intimately present to us, both in reality around us and in the secret of our heart. Each act of human choice reveals our ability to imitate divine creativity in the concrete. (Ingham, 2003, p. 38)

Scotus teaches that all things are contingent: that is, they do not exist out of necessity, but as a result of the free loving choice of God. The only necessary being is God, as the uncaused cause of all that exists; everything other than God exists as sheer gift. God didn't have to create the universe, but he wanted to in order to invite all things to share in the loving relationship pre-existing within the Holy Trinity. In creation there is no necessity, only grace, conferring the responsibility onto humanity of echoing that grace with our free response of love.

Relationship and delight in creation

The overflowing sense of delight in creation described by Bonaventure and Scotus is itself a typical feature of Franciscan spirituality. We have already seen in the first section of this book how Francis of Assisi delighted in the natural world. Bonaventure himself was deeply moved by the example of Francis, writing in his *Major Legend of Saint Francis*:

> From a reflection on the primary source of all things, filled with even more abundant piety, he would call creatures, no matter how small, by the name of 'brother' or 'sister', because he knew they shared with him the same beginning. (II.590)

Francis looked to God as the 'primary source' of all things; he lived the consequences of what had happened 'in the beginning', and what was always happening in every beginning, wherever Wisdom delighted to be. This beginning is not just the first item in a causal sequence, but a constant potentiality, ready to emerge into being whenever the divine Word is spoken and the Wisdom of God is expressed. This is known in Christian theology as 'continuous creation' (Latin *creatio continua*), the view that God is not a divine watchmaker, assembling the pieces of his creation, winding it up and letting it run, but rather God continually creates all things, holding them in being by his active compassion, never once leaving them to fend for themselves.

According to Bonaventure, it was this sense of the constantly refreshed fruitfulness of creation that filled Francis with 'piety'. In modern English usage this word has a faintly condescending tone, almost encouraging the addition of words like 'outdated' or 'exaggerated'; but the Latin term *pietas* meant rather the obligation that someone would have to a blood relation. Piety primarily referred to devotion to God, but was also used in the discourse of human relationships, with an emphasis on loyalty, courtesy and shared honour. Francis was respectful, courteous and caring to all creatures, not just the men who shared his social status: he called every creature 'brother' and 'sister' because they were all, in his eyes, members of one family. This kinship was rooted in their co-creation by God, acting with Wisdom, singing them into existence by God's Word. Bonaventure develops this thought:

> True piety, which according to the Apostle [St Paul] gives power to all things, had so filled Francis' heart and penetrated its depths that it seemed to have claimed the man of God completely into its dominion. This is what, through devotion, lifted him up into God; through compassion, transformed him into Christ; through self-emptying, turned him to his neighbour; through universal reconciliation with each thing, refashioned him to the state of innocence. Through this virtue he was moved with piety to all things, especially to souls redeemed by the precious blood of Jesus Christ. (II.586)

Here, Bonaventure links the word piety with devotion, compassion, self-emptying and reconciliation. This was the vocabulary of salvation for Bonaventure and his spiritual mentor Francis of Assisi – devotion to God, compassion for the suffering, and reconciliation with all. In this way he returned to 'the state of innocence': that is, to the primordial friendship with God and all things, as experienced in the garden of Eden.

In all this, Francis was being 'transformed into Christ', and this happened in both a spiritual and a physical way. Spiritually, he more and more entered into the mystery of Christ's sufferings, as St Paul wrote in his letter to the Philippians: 'I want to know Christ and the power of his resurrection and the sharing of his sufferings by becoming like him in his death, if somehow I may attain the resurrection from the dead' (Phil. 3.10–11). Compassion, literally suffering with another, was a hallmark of the spirituality of Francis. He lived it not just in his mind, but in his flesh. Physically, Francis became so emptied of self that his own body was conformed to that of Christ, finding in his hands, feet and side the wounds of the crucified Jesus literally formed, raw and bleeding. These 'stigmata', the signs of the passion of Christ, date from a retreat Francis made to La Verna in Umbria in 1224. It was then that he had a vision of a crucified seraph and received the wounds of Christ, which became the distinguishing feature of later artistic depictions of the saint. For Francis, reconciliation with God was found in union with Christ, and this in turn led to the desire for reconciliation with all in whom he discovered the saving presence of his Lord.

Angela of Foligno: 'This world is pregnant with God!'

A follower of Francis from the next generation wrote movingly of the discovery of the delightful presence of God in creation. This was Angela of Foligno (c.1248–1309), who was a member of the Franciscan Third Order, often known as Tertiaries. Some members of this Order belong to Third Order Regular communities and take the traditional vows of poverty, chastity and obedience; others, referred to in the Roman Catholic Church as the 'Secular' Franciscan Order, may be married or single, lay or ordained, interweaving into their lives the Franciscan values of simplicity, love and joy.

As a young woman, married and with four sons, Angela prayed that she might be released from her domestic responsibilities to spend more time in devotion to God and in service to those in need. Her prayer was answered in a more literal way than she could have expected when her husband and sons died in an outbreak of the plague. Subsequently she sold most of her possessions and together with a faithful companion she dedicated her life to Christ after the example of Francis of Assisi. In her *Book of the Blessed Angela of Foligno*, written with the help of a cousin who belonged to the Friars Minor, we can read the intimate history of a mystic going through the stages of a religious conversion, in great earnestness and purity of heart.

Evelyn Underhill, the Anglican pioneer of studies of mysticism, said of Angela in *The Mystics of the Church* that she was 'in many respects the most remarkable of the great Franciscan mystics' (Underhill, p. 99). More recently, Bernard McGinn, in his series on the history of Western Christian mysticism, speaks of Angela's *Book* as 'the premier text of all Franciscan women mystics', and her descriptions of union with God as 'one of the richest ... in Christian history' (McGinn, 1998, pp. 141, 145).

Angela itemized the many stages of her spiritual journey, and here she speaks of the Second Supplementary Step along the way:

> One day while I was in prayer and wanted to say the Our Father, suddenly my soul heard a voice which said: 'You are full of God.' I truly felt all the members of my body filled with the delights of God ... My companion, who saw the state I was in, said that tears were streaming from my eyes, which were wide open ... God replied: 'It is true that the whole world is full of me.' And then I saw that every creature was indeed full of his presence ... I saw a fullness, a brightness with which I felt myself so filled that words fail me, nor can I find anything to compare it with. (Angela, 1993, pp. 147–51)

This experience came to Angela as a complete surprise. She wasn't praying in a church or going on a pilgrimage, she was just lying down in her own room. It was a very physical experience for her: she tangibly felt filled with delight, and her eyes wept tears of gratitude. It was also an experience that she couldn't adequately explain in words – a theme she returns to often in her book – and you can imagine her sitting in the back of a church explaining all this to her friar cousin, as he tried desperately to keep up with the flow of her words as he wrote, translating from her Umbrian dialect into the more formal Latin of literary works. At first it was a personal experience of being herself filled with the presence of God, but gradually it opened out into the awareness that every creature is full of God, and that the whole world is radiant with the presence of God if only we had eyes to see.

In the Fourth Supplementary Step we read of another vision of the overwhelming presence of God in all things:

> Afterward he added, 'I want to show you something of my power.' And immediately the eyes of my soul were opened,

and in a vision I beheld the fullness of God in which I beheld and comprehended the whole of creation, that is, what is on this side and what is beyond the sea, the abyss, the sea itself, and everything else. And in everything that I saw, I could perceive nothing except the presence of the power of God, and in a manner totally indescribable. And my soul in an excess of wonder cried out, 'This world is pregnant with God!' Wherefore I understood how small is the whole of creation – that is, what is on this side and what is beyond the sea, the abyss, the sea itself, and everything else – but the power of God fills it all to overflowing. (Angela, 1993, pp. 169–70)

This has many similarities with the vision of the English woman known to us as Julian of Norwich (1342–1416), in which she sees the fragility and yet the stability of creation, as it is held forever in God's care:

In this vision [our Lord] also showed me a little thing, the size of a hazel-nut in the palm of my hand, and it was as round as a ball. I looked at it with my mind's eye and thought, 'What can this be?' And the answer came to me, 'It is all that is made.' I wondered how it could last, for it was so small I thought it might suddenly have disappeared. And the answer in my mind was, 'It lasts and will last for ever because God loves it; and everything exists in the same way by the love of God.' (Julian, 1998, p. 47)

Maybe Julian had read or heard of the *Book of the Blessed Angela of Foligno*, though it seems unlikely given the restrictions on the dissemination of ideas in an age before the printing press. The tone of each writer is subtly different. Julian writes with great delicacy and gentleness of the hazelnut nestling in the palm of God; Angela writes with characteristic energy and vivacity. Both writers, however, are confident enough of their intuitions to directly describe the mystery of God's presence in feminine terms. Angela, as a mother herself, describes the pregnancy of the world; Julian later in *Revelations of Divine Love* speaks with great tenderness of Jesus our mother, bringing us to birth and feeding us with the pure milk of his teaching.

One clear point of contact between Angela and Julian is their deep desire for union with God. Julian continues in the passage quoted above:

> But what [God] the maker, the carer and the lover really is to me, I cannot tell; for until I become one substance with him, I can never have complete rest or true happiness; that is to say, until I am so bound to him that there is no created thing between my God and me. (Julian, 1998, p. 47)

Julian longs to become 'one substance' with God, so much so that her hand holding the hazelnut becomes God's hand holding the universe; they are one body, with nothing in all creation to separate them from each other. God is still Julian's 'maker, carer and lover' (a refreshing translation of Father, Son and Holy Spirit), but God's love leads her to become one with God at the core of her being – or rather, to reveal the unity that has been hidden by the folly of humanity. These are themes that will re-emerge as we continue to learn from Angela of Foligno in the chapters below.

Both Angela and Julian find the compassion of God mirrored in the maternal love of humanity. The discovery of this love is by no means limited to our perception of the 'natural world'. Humanity is just as much part of nature as a forest or an ocean, and 'the power of God fills it all to overflowing'. This means that everything and everyone is a conduit of God: a river to irrigate our parched spirits, a well of wisdom to refresh our minds, a fountain (as Bonaventure would put it) of the fullness of God, raining down upon us God's blessings and delight. Just as Angela found everything 'pregnant with God' and rejoiced, so Francis found joy in all creation, but particularly in humanity, in the brothers God gave him, and the poor in whom he met his homeless Lord.

Angela of Foligno was not only a 'nature mystic' – someone who found God in the natural world – she also had powerful experiences of service to Christ in the poor and those in sickness. She recounts one such occasion in her Third Supplementary Step:

On Maundy Thursday, I suggested to my companion that we go out to find Christ: 'Let's go,' I told her, 'to the hospital and perhaps we will be able to find Christ there among the poor, the suffering and the afflicted.' ... And after we had distributed all that we had, we washed the feet of the women and the hands of the men. (Angela, 1993, pp. 162–3)

Reading this passage you can't help feeling a little sorry for Angela's companion. Every day she must have woken up with a sense of dread: 'What is Angela going to get up to today?' But in her dutiful loyalty she goes along with the day's adventure. Angela specifically focuses on finding Christ among the poor and destitute, probably having heard the stories of Francis working in leper houses, and sending his novices to such places to learn about the love of God. And she really throws herself into the experience. She goes out of her way to nurse one of the patients who was in a particularly bad state. This is experiencing the body of Christ in a whole new way, revealing to her the presence of Christ in the body of the sick, and subsequently in her own recoiling body. In this way Angela is a true disciple of Francis, whose turning point in his own life came when he physically embraced a man with leprosy, and so overcame his natural revulsion at this disease. Both Angela and Francis find in the embrace of the suffering other the experience that there is no 'other', no one who does not have a part to play in our life. Nothing is outside of the one suffering and salvific body of Christ.

Jacopone da Todi and Francisco de Osuna: finding God in all things

Another great mystic of the Franciscan tradition wrote poems and songs that expressed the depths and heights of the spiritual journey. *The Lauds* by Jacopone da Todi (*c.*1230–1306) were written in the Umbrian dialect of Italian, and form some of the earliest examples of poetry written in the language of the ordinary people of the day. He was a notary, a kind of lawyer who specialized in drawing up legal documents, but after the death of his wife in tragic circumstances he became a wandering ascetic who often flouted the conventions of society. Eventually he became a Franciscan friar, but retained his mischievous streak. His opposition to the election of Pope Boniface VIII in 1297 earned him a prolonged spell in prison, where he wrote some of his most eloquent songs or 'lauds', as well as revealing a dark but poignant sense of humour. Eventually he was released by Pope Benedict XI, but his broken health led to his death three years later in 1306.

In Laud 82, 'How the soul through the senses finds God in all creatures', there is a beautiful example of a Franciscan friar rejoicing in the presence of the living God:

From five sides You move against me,
Hearing, sight, taste, touch, and scent.
To come out is to be caught; I cannot hide from You.

If I come out through sight I see Love
Painted in every form and colour,
Inviting me to come to You, to dwell in You.

If I leave through the door of hearing,
What I hear points only to You, Lord;
I cannot escape Love through this gate.

If I come out through taste, every flavour proclaims:
'Love, divine Love, hungering Love!
You have caught me on Your hook,
For You want to reign in me.'

If I leave through the door of scent
I sense You in all creation; You have caught me
And wounded me through that fragrance.

If I come out through the sense of touch
I find your lineaments in every creature;
To try to flee from You is madness ...

If I see evil in a man or defect or temptation,
You fuse me with him, and make me suffer;
O Love without limits, who is it You love?
(Jacopone, 1982, pp. 239–40)

Jacopone talks of 'leaving through the sense doors' because at that time it was thought that when seeing, for example, some form of consciousness left from the eye and then returned, rather like modern-day radar. Maybe we do project our awareness into the awareness of others, our nervous systems creating a kind of pulsating electromagnetic field around us that others can intuitively sense.

Jacopone uses the image of being 'drawn out' by God when he would rather hide away in himself. But the self he tries to protect out of fear is drawn irresistibly to others in pain, and to Christ suffering on the cross. The poet feels the pain of abandoning his fortified self as he is lost in Christ, but realizes that this birth of compassion as he goes out to others is in fact his only means of healing. Jacopone finds that the beauty of nature is the lure that draws him to true safety, the hook that lands him on the shore of delight in God's presence. But as in the experience of Angela of Foligno, Jacopone meets Christ not only in the beauties of nature but also in the suffering of his fellow human beings. The awakening of his senses to the natural world opens the eyes of his heart to compassion. Like Francis, he cannot run away from the leper, but is 'fused' with the other man, and so is himself healed by the crucified Christ who loves without limits.

The writings of Jacopone are one of the largely unknown gems of the Franciscan spiritual tradition. McGinn says of him: 'His *Lauds* are astonishing in their range and their complexity of tone and message ... Jacopone's ability to suggest the annihilating power of the experience of divine love has few rivals in the history of Christian mysticism' (McGinn, 1998, p. 126). Only in the contemporary writings of the Beguine mystics of the Low Countries, and the German Dominican Meister Eckhart, are there comparable descriptions of the darkness of the divine abyss, and the irresistible gravity of God, like a black hole drawing everything into itself.

Further nuances on the Franciscan attitude to creation can be found in a later writer and teacher of prayer, Francisco de Osuna (1492–1540), in his book *The Third Spiritual Alphabet*. He called it an 'alphabet' because every chapter began with a short, pithy phrase summing up the contents of the chapter, each one beginning with a letter of the Spanish alphabet. Osuna was a Franciscan friar living in Spain, and his book was of great help to the famous Carmelite nun St Teresa of Avila. She read the book as a teenager, and said later that it taught her everything she needed to know about prayer. Her original copy, with copious notes and annotations, is still treasured at the convent in Spain where she lived. In the chapter entitled 'Apply love to everything and draw love from everything' (*'Referir y sacar deves do toda cosa el amor'*), Osuna writes:

> Since the cornerstone of this exercise is love for God, without which we cannot become perfectly recollected in him, it is absolutely necessary to expend all our energy to intensify this love so that we can be not only recollected but sealed in God. We are not distracted if we contemplate the universality of creatures in order to love God through them ... Fulfilling the counsel of our letter in this manner, you will return everything you see to its origin and acknowledge the way everything came to be, which was through powerful love. (Osuna, 1981, pp. 415–16)

Recollection, or as we might say these days, Christian mindfulness, is based on the love of God: finding God in all creation, that central pillar of Franciscan spirituality, and turning this joyful discovery into praise and blessing. It is about seeing all things in the light of their pristine wholeness and beauty as created by a loving God.

So in this chapter we have seen how the first followers of Francis responded to his message, living it out in their own situations. Clare, one of his first and most loyal supporters, renounced all wealth and security, trusting only in God, and was eventually granted the 'privilege of poverty'. Clare rejoiced in the natural world around her, but accepted only the least possible amount for herself and her sisters in community. Bonaventure and Scotus expressed in the theological language of their day how all things emerge from and return to God, rejoicing with Paul that 'from him and through him and to him are all things' (Rom. 11.36); and teaching that Christ, as the 'exemplar' of all things, holds all creation in being. We have seen how Francis responded to this loving Creator with great devotion, and in compassion for his fellow creatures, recognizing all as his sister and brother in the family of God. Moving on to the Franciscan mystics of the next generation we have seen how Angela of Foligno and Jacopone da Todi had powerful experiences of the presence of God, both in the 'natural world' and in people experiencing suffering. But this is not the end of the Franciscan way: now we must turn to the next stage of the journey, the adagio movement of God's symphony of creation, and open our ears and eyes to the experiences of loss that break open the shell of the well-defended soul.

Questions for reflection

- Where do you feel most strongly the presence of God: in a church, in the countryside, somewhere else?
- Do you find God in the people around you? If so, how?
- How might you practically enter into the service of others, and so serve Christ?

Further reading

Ilia Delio, 2003, *A Franciscan View of Creation: Learning to Live in a Sacramental World*, New York: The Franciscan Institute.
Sister Frances Teresa, 1995, *This Living Mirror: Reflections on Clare of Assisi*, London: Darton, Longman and Todd.
William Short, 1999, *Poverty and Joy: The Franciscan Tradition*, London: Darton, Longman and Todd.

6

Into the Dark

Franciscan theology certainly begins with a keen sense of the beauties of creation, and the blessing of God discovered in our fellow creatures, but the story doesn't end there. Creation and Fall follow one another like the footsteps in walking: a repeated sequence of the offer of grace and the turning away of humanity to sin. The story starts full of promise, but this soon turns to regret and the need for a fresh beginning offered by the ever resourceful and creative God.

'In the beginning': the book of Genesis

At first sight everything seems to be going well. In the account of the creation, in chapter 2 of the Book of Genesis, Adam is created first, and then every living creature, so that they might be 'a helper as his partner' (Gen. 2.18). Even though Adam names the creatures, establishing a relationship with them all, still the desired partner cannot be found. So God makes Eve, of whom Adam can say, 'This at last is bone of my bones and flesh of my flesh; this one shall be called Woman, for out of Man this one was taken' (Gen. 2.23). This story is about partnership, companionship and solidarity. Adam is made of the dust of the earth, suggesting the rootedness of humanity in the soil, sharing in its enrichment or impoverishment. He tills the ground, and shares by the sweat of his brow in the fate of the land.

In contrast, the story of creation given in the first chapter of Genesis strikes a note that in one respect at least is full of foreboding to our modern ears. Here the key verses for our purposes are Genesis 1.27–28:

So God created humankind in his image, in the image of God he created them; male and female he created them. God blessed them, and God said to them, 'Be fruitful and multiply, and fill the earth and subdue it; and have dominion over the fish of the sea and over the birds of the air and over every living thing that moves upon the earth.'

Here for many people is the smoking gun in the hand of the Judeo-Christian tradition – laying bare its responsibility for the ecological devastation that has disfigured the earth and destroyed so many natural habitats. The words 'subdue' (Hebrew *kabash*) and 'have dominion' (*radah*), sum up the violence of human domination, and make the Bible a charter for the denaturing of the earth and the root cause of the current climate emergency. Richard Bauckham, in his book *Bible and Ecology*, tries hard to see the redeeming elements of this passage, pointing out that the word 'subdue/*kabash*' is usually used in the Hebrew Bible for the action of occupying and taking possession of the land away from its previous occupants; the land itself is not the enemy to be subdued.

In Genesis 1.28 the land that is to be subdued is the same land that is to be filled by humans (i.e. all the land in the world), and the two actions are closely connected. It seems likely that subduing the land here refers to agriculture, since the only way humans are able to fill the land is to cultivate it and so to make it yield more food than it would of its own accord. As we have noted, the element of force may not be intrinsic to the verb *kabash*, but if it is, then the reference is to the fact that farmers must work the land to make it yield crops (Bauckham, 2010, p. 17).

As Bauckham goes on to point out, the vision of Genesis 1 is still a peaceful, non-violent scene where humanity, and indeed 'everything that has the breath of life' is as yet vegetarian. There may be domestic livestock for wool or milk, but no slaughter of animals for food, no hint of the factory farms to come.

But the Franciscan answer to this seeming call to dominion is plain to see in the great Canticle of the Creatures composed by Francis. There, as we have seen, he sings of 'our Sister Mother

Earth, who sustains and governs us'. It is the earth that governs us, has dominion over us, even if humanity likes to think it is in control. Rather should the followers of Francis be 'simple and subject to all', even to animals, and to their enemies, or the Saracens among whom they may choose to live (I.74, I.165).

Francis, Bonaventure, creation and sin

Francis emphasized the aspect of disobedience in his analysis of the Fall, saying in his *Admonitions*:

> [Adam] was able to eat of every tree of paradise, because he did not sin as long as he did not go against obedience. For that person eats of the tree of the knowledge of God who makes his will his own and, in this way, exalts himself over the good things the Lord says and does in him. (I.129)

The primary sin, for Francis, was a matter of disobedience, a turning away from the blessing of the Lord by claiming the credit for the good things God does through us. Francis admonishes his brothers that 'all creatures under heaven serve, know, and obey their Creator, each according to its own nature, better than you' (I.131). Creation naturally obeys the Creator; only humanity remains attached to its own will. In this way, obedience is an aspect of poverty, a letting go of self, and 'where there is poverty with joy, there is neither greed nor avarice' (I.137). Dispossession is a blessing, a relief for the giver as much as for the one who receives. On one of the many occasions Francis gave away his cloak to a poor person he said to his brothers: 'We must give back to this poor man the mantle that is his. We accepted it on loan until we should find someone poorer than we are' (II.139). For Francis, clinging to property was theft, while giving to another was true justice. Spiritual poverty was a way to joyfully trust in the abundant provision of God.

Above all, for Francis, obedience was a reciprocal honouring of one another. In his *Earlier Rule* of 1221 he wrote: 'Let no brother do or say anything evil to another; on the contrary, through the charity of the Spirit, let them serve and obey one another voluntarily. This is the true and holy obedience of our Lord Jesus Christ' (I.67).

Obedience was not about domination, or the reinforcing of hierarchy. Instead the brothers should obey one another, with the brother in charge being called 'guardian' rather than 'prior' (literally 'the first'), and the provincial leader being called the 'minister' as one who serves, rather than 'abbot' or 'superior' as was the case in other religious orders. The significance of this for us today is the insight that humankind fell from its original blessing when it lost sight of the importance of mutuality. According to Francis, happiness is not found in the amassing of temporal goods but in the rediscovery of the infinite bounty of God, and the inseparability of the needs of others from our own needs. When one suffers all suffer; when one facilitates the abundance of another, all are blessed. If the current crises of health and climate teach us anything, it is that we are all in this together. Our obedience is due to each other; there is no hope for us on our own.

As he begins his deliberations 'On the Corruption of Sin' in his *Breviloquium*, Bonaventure offers an olive branch of hope:

> What we must hold is summarized thus: sin is not some positive essence, but a defect, a corruptive tendency ... Hence the corruptive power of sin, while opposed to good as such, yet has no being except in a good, and no origin except from a good; which good is the will's capacity for free choice. And this capacity is not entirely evil, for it may tend toward good; nor entirely good, for it may fall into evil. (Bonaventure, 1963, p. 109)

In other words, sin is not all bad! At root, at least, there is good in everything. Here Bonaventure is following his mentor Augustine of Hippo, who taught that there was no parity between good and evil. Only good had true being; evil was just the corruption of a prior good. The analogy he used was of light and darkness: darkness was not a thing itself, merely the absence of light. Similarly, evil didn't exist in its own right, but was simply a privation of the good. This didn't mean that there was nothing wrong with the world – anyone could see that there was much needing to be put right – but the battle between good and evil was not in any way equally balanced. Good always had the upper hand.

In this teaching there are at least signs of a possible solution to the potential catastrophe of climate change. The current situation is rooted in a qualified good – the use of human ingenuity and technology to discover how to grow more food, heal more diseases, reduce the burden of labour and increase awareness of each other through social media. Development is not a bad thing; it just needs to be sustainable. The ingenuity that can turn sun, wind and wave power into an abundant, safe source of heat and light could ensure the availability of plentiful power that has no harmful destructive side effects, opening the possibility of a bountiful life for all.

For Bonaventure, the primal sin was one of inattention. Eve didn't keep her eye on the open book of the Wisdom of God (cf. Bonaventure, 1963, p. 115). There was nothing wrong with her 'judgment of reason' – she could read that book perfectly well – but she chose instead to look at the externals of the situation. Her choice of the perishable over the imperishable led to her downfall, just as the relentless search for material comfort in the world today can lead to loss of the divine wisdom that cherishes and protects the biodiversity of creation. Overconsumption is perhaps most clearly the cause of our critical situation today.

In all this, Eve may have been created after Adam, but she is at the forefront of the story. She is the one who makes all the running while Adam skulks around in the background.

In his excessive love for the woman's company and the solace of her presence, he shrank from reproving her lest he endanger his own happiness ... In both man and woman there occurred a disruption of order in all their powers, from the highest to the lowest: first in their intellect, then in their senses, and finally in their actions. Both fell into disobedience and succumbed to greed because both had risen in pride. (Bonaventure, 1963, pp. 116–17)

Here the fundamental sin of Adam is a curious one: he sinned because he didn't want to upset his wife and be denied his conjugal rights. Perhaps this is an indication of who ruled the roost in a thirteenth-century Italian household! But basically the fault is the same on both sides: pride leading to greed leading to disobedience; sins of the intellect, senses and actions.

The spiritual path and lament

This concentration on the Fall of humanity had many consequences, and was a theme beloved of medieval painters, often to be found in the 'doom' pictures covering the arch at the sanctuary end of a medieval church. These pictures resonated with Christians because they often felt themselves to be cast out of the delights of paradise, cursed to experience lives of hardship and toil, with the ever present threat of death by injury, illness or war. And for women there was the additional terror of death in childbirth. Such fears coloured everything, especially their experience of the natural world. The blame laid at the feet of the senses for their role in the catastrophe of the Fall made physical pleasure a dangerous precursor to suffering. For all their delight in the natural world, the Franciscan authors were just as wary of the senses as any other medieval Christian.

We have already shared in the delight of Jacopone da Todi in the senses, leading him to Christ. Here in Laud 27, 'The soul cries out for help against the senses', we see him in a more sombre mood:

O Blessed Christ, Love source of all delight,
Have pity on my wretchedness! ...

Help me escape from the deceitful Enemy, O Lord;
His arrows, shot from afar, are aimed at the cleansed heart.
I cannot see the hand that wounds me;
To suffer thus is more than I can bear ...

The nose seeks pleasure in scent,
The palate something good to taste;
And all the senses seek to make me
Subject to them. Nor are they satisfied
When I grant them what they want;
They complain bitterly at the skimpiness
Of the portion!
(Jacopone, 1982, pp. 118–19)

The medieval caricature of the corpulent Friar Tuck is far from the reality of the tortured soul of Jacopone. He is, it seems, on guard against almost everything: sights, sounds, smells, tastes, touch – all can be a snare to the unwary soul. It is as if, for Jacopone, the Fall is not just something that happened in a mythical past long ago. It is the turning away from God here and now, from relationship that gives us life, a turning away that happens in each person and for which we do penance.

In his own life Jacopone knew much suffering. He had been a successful lawyer, living a life of relative luxury for a man of his day. Then tragedy struck and his beloved wife was killed when the balcony on which she was standing with several others collapsed beneath them. On rushing to the scene and trying desperately to resuscitate his wife, Jacopone found underneath her expensive outer clothing a hair shirt, worn as a sign of a hidden life of penitence and prayer. Jacopone had known nothing about this devotion of his wife, and resolved as he held her dying body to live a life of penitence himself. Renouncing his occupation and joining the community of the Franciscan friars, his grief became his constant companion. He wrote and sang often of suffering and death, and the tragedy of an unfulfilled life, and his lauds became the signature tunes of the penitent movements sweeping Italy at the time, imploring God to have mercy before the inexorable visitation of death.

Jacopone is most eloquent when he talks about the loss of the sense of God's presence, after he has already had some experience of the love of God. In Laud 68 he laments:

Weep, my suffering soul,
Fallen into the hands of the Enemy,
For you are widowed of Christ's love!

Weep, suffer and sigh,
For you have lost your gentle Lord;
May these tears yet bring Him back
To my disconsolate heart ...

O my ears, why do you find solace
In the weeping of a grieving fellowship?
Do you no longer hear the voice of the Beloved
Who made you rejoice and break into song?

Oh, the sad, sad memories!
Harsh death gradually consumes me;
I am neither alive nor dead,
In torment, cut off from my Saviour.
(Jacopone, 1982, pp. 207–8)

Delight in creation is often seen as the hallmark of Franciscan spirituality, and it is true that this is an essential stage of the journey. But it is not the whole path. Experiences of loss and grief are almost bound to come as progressive waves of sorrow and joy wash over the soul like an ever returning relentless tide patiently polishing stones on a pebbled beach.

The spiritual path is sometimes divided into three aspects or phases: purgation, illumination and union. In purgation one becomes aware of one's sins and is spiritually cleansed by returning to God in repentance; in illumination, a new awareness of the overwhelming love of God begins to dawn; and in union one becomes united with the God of love. Bonaventure uses this classification in his book *The Triple Way*. But such stages in the spiritual life almost invariably appear on a cyclic basis: rarely is there an even progression from one stage to the next. More often, as seen explicitly in the *Book of the Blessed Angela of Foligno*, there is a multitude of stages, with the individual advancing and regressing in alternate states of

sorrow and joy, going through waves of consolation and desolation, to use the terms most familiar in the Ignatian tradition
of spirituality.

Darkness and spiritual poverty

Angela of Foligno herself had numerous 'moments of truth',
when the reality of her spiritual poverty broke through the
complacency that might have otherwise held her back. Often
she would meditate on the passion of Christ, a particular theme
associated with the Franciscans. It was they who popularized
the devotion known as The Stations of the Cross. Here the
devotee is led through the stages of the last day of the life of
Jesus, from the judgement at the hands of Pilate via the long,
painful journey carrying the cross-beam to the hill of Golgotha,
to death on the cross, and burial in a nearby tomb.

The Franciscan tradition is not just about the beauty of the
natural world. It also explores the darker side of life, and Angela
felt herself drawn to this kind of prayer. She experienced prolonged periods of despair in her spiritual life, despite the earlier
experiences of joy and consolation in the felt presence of God.
In the Sixth Supplementary Step, Arnaldo, her faithful scribe
and confidant, listens to his spiritual mentor as she describes
how she feels as if suspended in mid-air, with no means of
support, her sense of self-worth obliterated by demons:

> And when [my soul] perceives all its virtues being subverted
> and departing, and it can do nothing to prevent this process,
> the pain and the anger that it feels pushes it to such a point
> of despair that at times it cannot weep and at other times
> it weeps inconsolably. There are even times when I am so
> overwhelmed with rage that I can hardly refrain from tear-
> ing myself apart ... When my soul sees all its virtues fall and
> leave, then it is overcome with fear and grief. It wails and
> cries out to God repeatedly and unceasingly: 'My son, my
> son, do not abandon me, my son!' (Angela, 1993, pp. 197–8)

These are terrible words, and yet how modern they sound! This is not the bland reassurance that everything will be all right. Angela is full of pain, anger, even despair. She rages at God for allowing this to happen, for the way creation has become a closed book to her. Yet still she cries out as a parent, adapting the heartfelt grief of King David over his dead son Absalom (2 Sam. 19.4) to become her own motherly lament for the God who has deserted her and is as good as dead. Angela is in deep grief for the God she can no longer feel; she is in exile, cast out of the paradise of Eden she once shared with the Lord.

In our explorations of the theme of the Fall, we have first returned, as followers of Francis, to the Scriptures and the story of the Garden of Eden. Francis saw the Fall as a failure to enter the true spirit of freely chosen poverty and justice: the voluntary dispossession of all that holds us back from God, and the just redistribution of resources. Then Bonaventure guided us through his analysis of the Fall as a failure to read God's instruction manual, the book of creation, being distracted by material goods from the wisdom of God written within. Then our Franciscan companions Jacopone and Angela shared their experiences of despair and desolation, acknowledging that the stage of purgation returns even after periods of great spiritual consolation. In this way experiences of personal tragedy or spiritual darkness can alternate with times of refreshment and insight into the intimate union with Christ suffering and dying on the cross.

In our present crisis many feel an abiding sense of depression and anxiety: climate change, coronavirus, civil war and mass migrations of desperate refugees, all engender a sense of helplessness in the face of impending disaster. The world economic system seems unstoppable one day, then teetering on the edge of collapse the next. It sometimes feels like humanity is treading water in the ocean after a catastrophic shipwreck, holding hands with fellow survivors, and watching as the sharks circle, gathering for a feast. The question is more urgent than ever whether we will learn from this experience of the importance of cooperation and self-sacrifice. If ever we needed to learn the lesson of facing up to our self-inflicted exile from our planetary

Garden of Eden, now is the time. Is there a grain of hope in the Franciscan tradition to inspire us to rediscover and cherish the blessings of the creation, to see all things differently, with the eyes of the soul?

Questions for reflection

- Have you experienced times of darkness in your spiritual journey?
- How has the Covid-19 pandemic affected your faith?
- Are you hopeful or anxious about the future of our planet? Why?

Further reading

Angela of Foligno, 1993, *Angela of Foligno: Complete Works*, trans. Paul Lachance OFM, New York: Paulist Press.

Richard Bauckham, 2010, *Bible and Ecology: Rediscovering the Community of Creation*, London: Darton, Longman and Todd.

Ilia Delio, 2001, *Simply Bonaventure: An Introduction to His Life, Thought, and Writings*, New York: New York City Press.

7

The Journey Home

So far in our explorations of the rich world of the Franciscan relationship with creation we have seen the hallmark of joy, as the followers of Francis rejoice in the beauty of the created world. Here the senses are alive to the many communications of the presence of God, who is both 'with' all things and 'in' all things. This is perhaps the most well-known aspect of the life and teachings of Francis and of his followers over the subsequent centuries.

Then we looked at the experience of the loss of such feelings, and of the depth of despair that such experiences can evoke. Here creation has been superseded by the Fall, and humanity is driven out of paradise. This echoes so much of our experience today. Now we might say that the Fall of humanity has been the result not of the eating of a single apple, but of the mass destruction of forests across the globe. Is there a way forward, a further step in the journey of faith that will give us the possibility, at least, of reseeding our garden of delight?

Reconciliation, peace and the healing of the world

First, to return to Francis. At the end of his life, Francis reflected one last time on the most important discoveries he had made in his life, and had them written in a document known as his *Testament*. In this document he said nothing about finding God in preaching to birds, but he did talk about finding God in suffering human beings. This is how he began his *Testament*:

The Lord gave me, Brother Francis, thus to begin doing penance in this way: for when I was in sin, it seemed too bitter for me to see lepers. And the Lord himself led me among them and I showed mercy to them. And when I left them, what had seemed bitter to me was turned into sweetness of soul and body. And afterwards I delayed a little and left the world. (I.124)

This was a crucial turning point in the conversion of Francis, a moment when the Wisdom of God came to him and revealed her presence, when Christ spoke to him and made him whole. It was mercy – compassionate action on behalf of the sick and poor – that turned his world around. His senses were reversed like the poles of a magnet: what had once made him flee was now to draw him irresistibly nearer. Everything he relished before he now found empty; everything he had avoided now opened up into opportunities to share practically in the love of Christ. He says that he 'left the world', but this was just the expression used at the time to mean leaving lay life and joining a religious order. Francis didn't have to leave the world to find God, as if God were not there in the world already. Christ was everywhere for Francis, but he didn't fully realize that until he began to surrender anything that might separate him from those in whom he discovered Christ.

The return to the experience of oneness with God and with the whole of creation was rooted in the experience of reconciliation, of rediscovering the image and likeness of God in others. Francis began each sermon with the greeting: 'May the Lord give you peace!' (I.126, I.203, II.84) We have already seen how he wove an exhortation to peace into his Canticle of the Creatures, composing a stanza of the song to reconcile the bishop and the mayor of Assisi: 'Praised be You, my Lord, through those who give pardon for Your love, and bear infirmity and tribulation. Blessed are those who endure in peace for by You, Most High, shall they be crowned' (I.114).

It was as though his hymn of creation wasn't complete until it included a reference to the reconciliation of humanity; pardon and peace are key words in the vocabulary of Francis.

One of the earliest accounts of the beginnings of the Franciscan Order gives this summary of the message of Francis:

> For the great desire of blessed Francis was that he, as well as his brothers, would abound in such good deeds for which the Lord would be praised. He used to tell them, 'As you announce peace with your mouth, make sure that greater peace is in your hearts. Let no one be provoked to anger or scandal through you, but may everyone be drawn to peace, kindness and harmony through your gentleness. For we have been called to this: to heal the wounded, bind up the broken, and recall the erring.' (II.102)

Although the followers of Francis became known as great preachers of the word, Francis wanted them rather to be renowned for the goodness of their lives and the purity of their hearts. He knew that actions speak louder than words, and often the actions that speak loudest are those that reveal the integrity of a life lived in simplicity and joy. This was revealed most clearly in his desire to reconcile others, to make peace. Even 'sister death' became his welcomed friend, and the burning of 'brother fire', when used to cauterize at a physician's hand, was accepted with a courteous greeting (II.566). In the end, Francis had no enemies, except perhaps his own 'brother body', and he was a little ashamed that he had treated his body so harshly throughout his ascetic life (II.383). Towards his brothers he recommended only love, never grumbling or detracting from others. Above all such love should be practically expressed, as he says in *The Earlier Rule*:

> Let the brothers love one another, as the Lord says: This is my commandment: love one another as I have loved you. Let them express the love that they have for one another by their deeds, as the Apostle says: Let us not love in word or speech, but in deed and truth. (I.72)

Love, in deed and truth, was the evangelistic strategy of Francis, for the healing of the world.

Creation and contemplation: participating in all things

The breaking down of barriers between people, and the direct realization that suffering and joy overlap individuals in the love of God, were also clearly experienced by Jacopone da Todi. He writes of the stages of divine love in Laud 80:

> When the soul is in harmony with conscience
> It takes joy in the love of its neighbour.
> Then without doubt it is true love,
> Then we can call it charity.
>
> Love then joins the lover
> To his suffering brethren;
> And in his compassion he suffers more
> Than the man whose suffering he shares.
> (Jacopone, 1982, p. 235)

Jacopone calls this the third stage of divine love. It is reached after love has been firmly founded on the 'ordering of the senses' by obedience to reason. Only when 'the house is still and quiet', the heart stilled and made attentive by prayer, can the conscience resolve how to act in love. Francis experienced this when he realized that the pain of the leper was not something to avoid, but an invitation to embrace. The only way for both men to be healed was to discover their unity in the love of God.

Such a reversal of perception, a radical conversion of heart, was described at length in some of the last poems that Jacopone wrote. He was coming to the end of his life, his health having been broken by years languishing in prison for his opposition to the pope. But rather than dwelling in bitterness his heart sings with joy. In Laud 90, he takes the initiate further into the secrets of union with Love:

> For heaven and earth and all things created
> Cry out insistently that I should love:

'Make haste to embrace the Love
That made us all, love with all your heart!
Because that Love so desires you
He uses all things to draw you to Himself.'
I see all goodness and beauty and gentleness
Spilling out of this superabundance of holy light ...

Once I spoke, now I am mute;
I could see once, now I am blind.
Oh, the depths of the abyss in which,
Though silent, I speak; fleeing, I am bound;
Descending, I rise; holding, I am held;
Outside, I am within; I pursue and am pursued.
Love without limits, why do You drive me mad
And destroy me in this blazing furnace?
(Jacopone, 1982, pp. 259, 261)

With a string of paradoxes Jacopone tries to express the inexpressible. Goodness, beauty and gentleness shine out of everything like a blazing fire, but the poet is made blind and deaf and mute by the intensity of the divine love. It is as though he has stared into the sun and been driven out of his mind. Like an Indian *rag*, a classical musical form played on a sitar, the poem builds to a crescendo where the poet is lost in devotion to 'Love, Love-Jesus': '*Amor, amor Iesu*' in the Italian of the original. All sense of separation has been lost, and he has not just put on Christ as a garment, but has been drowned and consumed by Christ's love. Jacopone is like a Sufi mystic in Islam, such as his contemporary Jelaluddin Rumi, both chanting the divine names in their self-abandonment to God, in whose all-encompassing love they dissolve without fear.

Again in Laud 91, 'Self-annihilation and charity lead the soul to what lies beyond knowledge and language', Jacopone continues to speak the unspeakable:

Love beyond all telling, goodness beyond imagining,
Light of infinite intensity glows in my heart.

I once thought that reason
Had led me to You,
And that through feeling
I sensed Your presence,
Caught a glimpse of You in similitudes,
Knew You in Your perfection.
I know now that I was wrong,
That that truth was flawed ...

In God the spiritual faculties
Come to their desired end,
Lose all sense of self and self-consciousness,
And are swept into infinity ...

Participating in the essence of all creatures
[The soul] can now say, 'All things are mine.'
The doors open wide, and entering within
The soul becomes one with God,
Possesses what He possesses. It hears
What it did not hear, sees what it did not know,
Possesses what it did not believe,
Savours that which has no taste ...

The base of this highest of peaks is founded on *nichil*
Shaped nothingness, made one with the Lord.
(Jacopone, 1982, pp. 265–71)

Here, reason and feeling, catching glimpses of the presence of
God, are relinquished in the loss of self-consciousness as the
soul 'drowns' in the immensity of God. The soul no longer
appreciates the creation from a distance, or sees God in 'similitudes', but actively 'participates' in all things, knowing them
as part of this new, all-encompassing sense of self. The loss of
the delights of the bodily senses are as we already saw in the
section on the Fall; but here it is love that has taken the lead
and drawn the poet beyond physical sensation to the spiritual
senses, the senses of the soul. The soul in prayer 'hears what it
did not hear, sees what it did not know ... savours that which
has no taste'.

Creation and contemplation: the sense of the spirit

Teaching on the spiritual senses awakened in prayer was not an innovation of the Franciscans, even if they did make it an important part of their approach to the understanding of God and creation. Gregory of Nyssa (c.330–c.395) describes the function of the eyes of the soul in this way:

> When someone whose mind is but partially developed sees something clothed in some semblance of beauty, he believes that this thing is beautiful in its own nature ... but someone who has purified the eyes of his soul and is trained to see beautiful things ... makes use of the visible as a springboard to rise to the contemplation of the spiritual. (Clément, 1993, p. 218)

Direct communion with God is facilitated by the 'hidden eyes of the soul', a practice based on what was known to the Greek theologians of the early Church as *physike theoria* – 'knowledge of creatures' or 'contemplation of nature' (Clément, 1993, p. 213). The physical is symbolic of the spiritual, manifesting the eternal in time; likewise, the spiritual is the source of the physical, its inner core and meaning. In this way the contemplation of God is not an abstraction from creation, but a celebration of creation, and salvation is experienced by body, mind and spirit simultaneously.

In the Western Church, Gregory the Great (540–604), writing in his *Dialogues*, which would have been well known to Franciscan scholars of the thirteenth century, also refers to the spiritual senses. Gregory writes of St Benedict, who had a vision of the whole world being gathered up into a single ray of sunlight:

> The light of interior contemplation in fact enlarges the dimensions of the soul, which by dint of expanding in God transcends the world. Should I say this? The soul of the contemplative transcends itself when, in God's light, it is transported beyond itself. (Clément, 1993, p. 225)

Gregory says that in this new way of seeing, creation is not con-tracted or in any way demeaned. Rather, the soul is expanded and is enabled to encompass all things with the compassion-ate regard of God. Contemplation does not belittle the created world, drawing the attention away to something abstract and remote; rather, it expands the soul of the seer, giving a glimpse of the creation from the viewpoint of eternity. This is a differ-ent way of seeing, a heightening of the senses, a clarity of vision, a sharpening of the intuitive awareness.

These new faculties of the soul discovered in prayer are hinted at by Clare of Assisi in one of her letters to Blessed Agnes of Prague:

> Place your mind before the mirror of eternity!
> Place your soul in the brilliance of glory!
> Place your heart in the figure of the divine substance!
> And through contemplation,
> transform your entire being into the image
> of the Godhead itself,
> so that you too may feel what friends feel
> as they taste the hidden sweetness
> that, from the beginning,
> God himself has reserved for his lovers.
> (Armstrong, 2006, p. 51)

Here sight, touch and taste are all experienced in a spiritual way in the transformative experience of contemplative prayer. It was this experience that flowed out of Clare as she served her sisters in their frailty and sickness – a theme returned to again and again by her sisters in their testimonies at the Process of Canonization (e.g. Armstrong, 2006, p. 147). In her fourth letter to Agnes, Clare talks of feeling the touch, even smelling the fragrance of the divine lover, Christ. Prayer is for Clare not a dry, disembodied activity, but one in which every aspect of her physicality is subsumed into spiritual relationship with the Lord. As a true Franciscan, Clare is not transported out of this world, but discovers God in this very world, her senses height-ened and transformed.

This intensification of consciousness is aided by restraint of the physical senses – the traditional disciplines of fasting, silence and solitude that come under the heading of the purgative stage of the spiritual life. Such disciplines were the daily practice of Clare and her sisters. They lead not to a restriction but a release of the spirit, an intensification of awareness, an opening of the ears and eyes of the spirit, in which the beauty of all things and all people are clearly revealed. This is seeing from the inside out, not from the outside in: seeing directly the vast interconnected web of creation; not using it as a resource to exploit or even an object to save, but recognizing ourselves as part of this mystery of the infinite creativity of God. In this way we begin to place our mind in the 'mirror of eternity', in the words of Clare of Assisi: seeing with the eyes of Christ, the image of God and sustainer of the universe; allowing our entire being to be transformed into that image through contemplation.

Reading of experiences like this it is tempting to think that all this is meant for others, not for ourselves. When prayer times, if they happen at all, are a battle just to stay awake and keep focused, and when the day's responsibilities are overwhelming, where is the delight or comfort of prayer? Sitting at the back, or the front, of a church is more often cold and uncomfortable, not full of fire or delight. But the awakening of the spiritual senses can be a gradual awakening nurtured over a lifetime of patient commitment to prayer. It is not an escape to an other-worldly bliss, but a gradually dawning realization that this world is itself the kingdom of God. It is an invitation to delight in the flesh and blood reality of God's presence in this world.

When visitors to the monastery where I live first enter the chapel, they often remark on the tangibility of the stillness. This is in itself an awakening of a spiritual sense. It is rooted in a hundred years of faithful reading and recitation of the Scriptures, daily celebration of the Eucharist, and the silent prayers of thousands of visiting guests. We who live here are just curators of silence, custodians of a sacred space.

Creation and contemplation: darkness and nothingness

For Jacopone da Todi, having nothing and being nothing are central to the experience of prayer, for it is in this way – the surrender of self – that one enters into union with the God who is not a thing, but Being itself. The use of the term *nichil*, 'nothingness', seen in the above quotation from Laud 91, is found in another contemporary writer, Marguerite Porete, who died just a few years after Jacopone. Marguerite was a Beguine, a member of a religious community of laywomen: not strictly nuns belonging to one of the established orders, but independent women supporting themselves economically by handicrafts and devoting themselves to a life of prayer. She delights in the paradoxes of contemplative prayer in which the soul empties itself of itself and is filled with the mystery of God who is nothing, no-thing, and therefore not separate from the soul:

> I am what I am, says this Soul, by the grace of God. Therefore I am only that which God is in me, and not some other thing. And God is the same thing that He is in me, for nothing is nothing. Thus He is Who is. Therefore I am not, if I am, except what God is, and nothing is beyond God. I do not find anything but God, in whatever part I might find myself, for He is nothing except Himself, to speak the truth. (Porete, 1993, p. 145)

This is a passage that needs to be read several times before it yields up its meaning! Marguerite talks of the 'annihilated life', a life lost in the Love that is God, in which the soul has freely surrendered its own will to do only the will of God as far as it is able. The 'emptiness' of God and the nothingness of the soul coalesce, with no way of saying where one ends and the other begins. Marguerite experiences this as a great joy, as she surrenders herself to God, and as a great security for having nothing, being nothing, she has nothing to lose. With great delight she is melted and dissolved in Love.

But this was dangerous talk, and Marguerite was suspected of heresy. Despite her book being assessed and exonerated by two Dominican theologians, she was told by the church authorities to burn all copies and speak no more of her experiences in prayer. Marguerite refused, and was burnt at the stake in 1310.

Giving a further Franciscan take on this *via negativa*, this 'negative way' into the heart of union with God, we can do no better than return to the Franciscan mystic Angela of Foligno, speaking of her Seventh Supplementary Step:

> Afterward, I saw God in a darkness, and in a darkness precisely because the good that he is, is far too great to be conceived or understood ...
>
> No matter how far the soul or heart expands itself, all that expanse is less than this good. What I related until now – that is when the soul sees all creation overflowing with God's presence, when it sees the divine power or the divine wisdom (all of which Christ's faithful had said she had already seen in such a marvellous and indescribable way) – all this is inferior to this most secret good, because this good which I see with darkness is the whole, and all other things are but parts. (Angela, 1993, pp. 202–3)

Here Angela is not afraid to offer a critique of the 'typical' Franciscan experience of finding God in all things. This 'secret good' of seeing God 'in a darkness' is greater than any of the more outwardly conventional experiences of God's presence. Maybe this is an encouragement to those who also experience God as a darkness or emptiness in our own day. St Paul may write to the Romans that 'ever since the creation of the world [God's] eternal power and divine nature, invisible though they are, have been understood and seen through the things he has made' (Rom. 1.20), yet for many people God's presence and power are not self-evident. 'Where is God?' many people ask, and if God is here, why does the world continue to be so full of suffering and despair? Angela has been through her share of suffering and despair, and has come out the other side with an unshakeable faith in the God whom she meets in interior darkness, not light.

Although Angela is deeply convinced that this is a genuine experience of God, still she does not scorn the ordinary 'means of grace' as found in the sacraments. She meets the Creator God in this extension of the incarnation, this moment of eternity breaking into time. Like Francis her patron, she delights in the discovery of God in the host as it is consecrated and elevated in the celebration of the Mass. This is often the time when she has ecstatic visions of the closeness of God and the intimate mutual indwelling of the Lord and the spouse, Christ and the believer as one body in God's Spirit.

The journey into God

Such an ultimate reconciliation is hinted at by Bonaventure in his summary of the spiritual life, *The Soul's Journey into God.* Bonaventure wrote this treatise two years after being elected as Minister General of the Franciscan Order of Friars Minor, during a retreat at the hermitage of La Verna where Francis had received the wounds of Christ imprinted in his body. Bonaventure was looking for peace in the midst of a busy life of administrative responsibilities and crisis management within the Order. He wanted to reconnect with the authentic spirit of Francis, and to put into one text all that would be necessary to walk the spiritual path to unity with God.

In the course of this text he speaks of discovering the vestiges, the footprints of God, through and in the material creation, then in the human mind as formed in the image of God, and finally above itself in categories of the Good, and Being itself. He then seeks to transcend all workings of the human mind and spirit, passing over all things so as to find Christ the Way and the Door, the ladder into God. This was what he believed Francis had been able to do during his own retreat on Mount La Verna in 1224, two years before his death, as he received the sacred stigmata. This would be a mystical and secret discovery, unknown except to those who enter the fire of the Holy Spirit:

Since, therefore, in this regard nature can do nothing and effort can do but little, little importance should be given to inquiry, but much to unction; little importance should be given to the tongue, but much to inner joy; little importance should be given to words and to writing; but all to the gift of God, that is, the Holy Spirit; little or no importance should be given to creation, but all to the creative essence, the Father, Son and Holy Spirit. (Bonaventure, 1978, pp. 113–14)

This seems a strange place for a Franciscan to be ending his journey: 'little or no importance should be given to creation, but all to the creative essence'. But this is his conviction: nature alone cannot save us, only grace; creation alone is ultimately powerless, but the creative essence of God is irresistible. Franciscan spirituality is not in the end about the apotheosis of creation, or a return to the 'natural world'; rather it is about rediscovering the Spirit of God that we nonetheless meet in creation, in the human mind and heart. It is the simple perception of goodness and the delight of rediscovering the source of all being. And where is this to be found? What is the final word of Francis and his disciple Bonaventure?

But if you wish to know how these things come about, ask grace not instruction, desire not understanding, the groaning of prayer not diligent reading, the Spouse not the teacher, God not man, darkness not clarity, not light but the fire that totally inflames and carries us into God. (Bonaventure, 1978, p. 115)

These are all values upon which Bonaventure has based his whole life: instruction, understanding, reading, teaching, the clarity of the human mind. But here he says, all this has to be put to one side. We can hear in this the echo of St Paul writing to the Philippians, after enumerating all his qualifications as an observant, zealously religious man: 'Yet whatever gains I had, these I have come to regard as loss because of Christ. More than that, I regard everything as loss because of the surpassing value of knowing Christ Jesus my Lord' (Phil. 3.7–8). And this is where Bonaventure ends:

Let us, then, die and enter into the darkness; let us impose silence upon our cares, our desires and our imaginings. With Christ crucified let us pass out of this world to the Father so that when the Father is shown to us, we may say with Philip: *It is enough for us.* Let us hear with Paul: *my grace is sufficient for you.* Let us rejoice with David saying: *My flesh and my heart have grown faint; You are the God of my heart, and the God that is my portion forever. Blessed be the Lord forever and all the people will say: Let it be; let it be. Amen.* Here ends the soul's journey into God. (Bonaventure, 1978, p. 116)

This is where it ends: with Christ on the cross, passing over to God the Father; finding Christ in a suffering world where the creation itself cries out for the revelation of humanity as true children of God. Not leaving the world behind, but passing through death to new life; no longer exploiting creation, but rising to new life in Christ dedicated to the well-being of everything that lives. This is the way of seeing differently, opening our spiritual eyes to see the beauty and fragility of the created world. Perhaps this is a journey we have only just begun.

Questions for reflection

- Where is reconciliation most in need in our world today?
- Have you had experiences of the 'spiritual senses'? How could they be developed?
- How can doubt be a useful tool in the journey into God?

Further reading

Helen Julian CSF, 2020, *Franciscan Footprints: Following Christ in the ways of Francis and Clare*, Abingdon: Bible Reading Fellowship.
Jacopone da Todi, 1982, *Jacopone da Todi: The Lauds*, trans. Serge and Elizabeth Hughes, New York: Paulist Press.
Richard Rohr OFM, 2014, *Eager to Love: The Alternative Way of Francis of Assisi*, London: Hodder and Stoughton.

Franciscans and Creation Today

SAMUEL DOUBLE

8

Delight

[Francis] rejoices in all the works of the Lord's hands and through their delightful display he gazes on their life-giving reason and cause. In beautiful things he discerns Beauty Itself. (II.353)

The immediate context in which I write is the coronavirus pandemic, reaching its peak in London as I sit at my desk. In this situation of lockdown, it might be argued that concern for climate change, loss of biodiversity and problems of pollution take second place to loss of life, anxiety about the world economy, and the huge shock to our worldview that the infection is causing. At present we don't know how long the crisis will last or what its full effect will be on our lives in the years ahead. However, what we do know is that our vulnerability to this virus and the disruption it is causing are closely linked to the way of life that has developed and spread throughout our world over the past 50 years.

This has been a period during which the human population has expanded rapidly and has been heavily encroaching upon the habitats of other creatures, so increasing the risk of a crossover of viruses from them. Finance and industries have become no longer rooted in communities of place, and air travel has made the world small. Added to this, war, famine and oppression have led to some 60 million people seeking refuge in places other than where they were born.

Along with great benefits to the human household such as industrial production, advances in technology, and extension of life expectancy, there have been great costs: the plunder of the natural world, diminishment of biodiversity, and the pollution of water, land and atmosphere. Burning fossil fuels has increased the level of carbon dioxide in the atmosphere which is responsible for global warming and an increasingly unstable climate. Most serious of all perhaps has been the loss by the majority of the world's human population of any understanding that we belong to 'the household of creation'. We have become ignorant of the fact that we are completely dependent on other members of the household, non-human as well as human, for our well-being and even our survival, a point emphasized by the current worldwide pandemic.

Sadly, Christians too have often lost a sense of interdependency within the 'household of creation'. The fifth Mark of Anglican Mission is 'To strive to safeguard the integrity of creation and sustain and renew the life of the earth'. Many Anglicans, including those preparing for ordained ministry at St Mellitus College (a theological institute based in London and elsewhere where I teach regularly), focus heavily on the first four Marks of Mission – proclamation of the gospel, nurturing believers, serving those in need, and transforming society. Some, however, are less enthusiastic when it comes to the fifth mark: in fact, the students can be surprised that the care of creation is counted as 'mission' at all. Many assume that this is a niche interest, of concern to those who have a 'green' agenda, and that it has little to do with the Church's core Christian life. Some, indeed, are suspicious of a subject that seems to them to lean towards a pagan worship of nature.

From within the Franciscan tradition, I teach that a theology of creation is foundational to the rest of Christian theology. As we have seen in Bonaventure's writings, creation is the means of God's self-revelation, which finds its fulfilment in the incarnation. The fifth Mark of Mission in fact should be the first. I also teach that the call to action, heard by Francis in the little church of San Damiano near Assisi, to 'repair my house which as you see is all being destroyed', is urgent for these times.

Our book's final third (Chapters 8 to 10) is rooted in my experience as a Franciscan friar at Hilfield Friary in Dorset, where I have lived for many years, and now at our friary at Plaistow in east London. I explore how this experience, within our contemporary context, and that of other Franciscans, can inform theological, moral and spiritual understandings as part of Christian living. The challenge to all humanity, and particularly to Christians, is to see all creation differently and then to act to reconcile human life in all its many forms with God's gift of the created world.

In this chapter we consider how Francis' sacramental seeing and inhabiting of the world around him can transform our relationship with creation and also our self-understanding.

Attending

We were on the north bank of the Thames at Gallions' Reach, near the former Royal Docks' eastern entrance, now site of London City airport. I was with my friend Bob Gilbert, a writer and broadcaster on the natural life of the city, with whom I spend a day every couple of months walking through different parts of London. We were on a search for the Deptford Pink, a rare form of the dianthus family found at only 15 sites in England. It's misnamed because apparently there's no connection with Deptford, an area south of the river some distance from Gallions' Reach. We were walking a mile or so downriver from the Thames Barrier, erected in the 1980s to control exceptional tidal surges and to prevent the river in central London overflowing its banks. At this point the blocks of flats now rising on derelict dockland are protected by a concrete wall with a six-foot drop to the tidal foreshore below, which is where Bob told me that some time before he had seen the plant that he wanted to show me. Scaling the wall was made possible by an iron ladder in place on both sides, feasible for the two of us but a problem for Ash, Bob's rescued greyhound, who always comes with us on these outings. We decided that I would get over first and that Ash would then be handed to me below so that, reaching out my arms, I could catch him. Ash seemed very uncertain about the wisdom of this operation, with a look on his face as Bob lifted him over that might have said, 'Are you serious about this?' I did manage to catch him, but despite his streamlined racing slimness, his weight resulted in both of us splayed on the ground. 'And how are you going to get me back?' I could almost hear him thinking.

This part of the adventure over, we made our way through the line of plastic washed up by the high tide. Eventually we found what we were looking for: a small patch of deep pink flowers with delicate pale spots on slender stems that seemed to be thriving in this rather unlikely situation. There we sat beside the river among the flotsam; we ate our sandwiches and talked about plants, their presence in particular places and their persistence. I treasure these outings with Bob because he opens my eyes; he points out to me the gifts that I would never have seen without him. It's not just the rare flowers that I'm introduced to on these walks, it's the trees along the streets, the weeds in the pavement, the birds, the invertebrates and their stories – where they arrived from and how they come to be established there. We have seen avocets in East India Dock Basin, and watched and waited for the kingfisher on the banks of the River Lea which flows into the Thames and divides our borough of Newham from the neighbouring Tower Hamlets. In the bushes beside the river at Canning Town, we have heard the sharp song of the shy Cetti's Warbler. I'm learning to pay attention and to delight in the gifts around me in the city.

The prophets of the Old Testament were often known as 'seers' (1 Sam. 9.9): people who had both sight and insight, who not only observed what was around them in the world, but could also recognize significance in what they saw. The prophets Amos and Jeremiah especially had the gift of reading the book of creation, of seeing into the life of the natural world and understanding what was being said by God to them and to the people (Amos 8.2; Jer. 1.11). What comes across clearly in the early writings about Francis that were explored in the first part of this book is that he, too, was a seer in this sense. He possessed the gift of keen observation of the creatures around him – their presence, their colours, their songs and their patterns of behaviour, and what he saw often brought him joy and delight. But his appreciation was not principally aesthetic, nor was his perception just sentimental or idealistic – in fact he had a critical opinion of certain animals. Rather, his delight in what he observed led him to see in the natural world around him, both animate and inanimate, the 'footprint' of the Creator, the maker's mark, a sign of God's mercy, generosity, love and glory. This in turn led him to thanksgiving and praise. Among those who came after Francis in the thirteenth century, Angela of Foligno, recognizing every creature as 'full of God's presence', and the world as 'pregnant with God', also has this sacramental approach. The same goes for John Duns Scotus, for whom every creature in its unique 'this-ness' points towards Christ, the masterpiece of God's creation.

The ecological crisis we face is due largely to the way we see, or rather, the way we *don't* see the world around us. In the life of our Western developed culture we are often too busy, travelling too fast, and too distracted to pay the sort of attention that Francis gave to the created world. Like those of whom Elizabeth Barrett Browning wrote in the middle of the nineteenth century, we are blind to the sacramental presence of what is before our eyes:

Earth's crammed with heaven,
And every common bush afire with God:
But only he who sees, takes off his shoes,
The rest sit round it, and pluck blackberries.

Bonaventure ascribes the Fall to the failure to read the manual of creation in which every creature is a word of God. For him, sin is essentially inattention. Our inattention to creation has increased over the past hundred or so years, paradoxically in part because our means of seeing has increased so much. The development of communications technology has widened our horizons and has opened to us the wonders of creation – for example, Sir David Attenborough's BBC TV series *Planet Earth*, in which he communicates a breathless excitement over what he is showing us. Yet seeing something on television is not the same as being present to it in person. So much of our perception of the world now comes to us mediated via a screen that our sight is often distracted from what is immediate to us. How can you notice the glory of the sunset if your eyes are fixed on your phone? How can you hear the wind in the poplar trees if you are plugged into earphones? And how, if you are texting your friend in Aberdeen as you walk along the road, can you notice the homeless person squatting on the pavement? Would Francis have noticed the leper if he had had a smartphone in his hand?

It would have been good if the *Planet Earth* series, as well as showing us some stunning film of tropical rainforests, deserts and oceans, had also pointed us to what is in our own garden or backyard. According to a State of Nature Report in 2019 (National Biodiversity Network), there has been a decline of 41 per cent in abundance and 27 per cent in distribution of animal species across the UK since 1970. Although this has been offset to some extent by increases in certain species, it represents a very significant loss: when did we last hear a cuckoo or spot a hedgehog around our gardens? Sadly, this loss has gone largely unnoticed by the majority of a population too busy and pre-occupied to give it their attention. Seeing needs commitment and disciplined attention. It also requires us to slow down.

Perhaps Francis' gift of 'reading' creation developed because for most of his life, until he became frail and sick and allowed himself to be borne by a donkey, he travelled everywhere on foot. Four-legged transport was for the rich and powerful, not for himself and his brothers. It's not long ago from our own generation that the daily walk to work, to the shops or to school was what everyone experienced: most people beyond our affluent world still walk in this way. Only recently in the span of human history have we become addicted to travelling in metal boxes or tubes for ease and comfort, and to enable us to get wherever we are going faster.

Walking slows us down. It limits us, and can open our eyes and ears, in fact all our senses, to what is before us: the lie of the land, the fold of hills, the shapes of trees and buildings. Through walking we feel the wind on our faces and hear the sound of birdsong. It connects us with our bodies. It gives us a sense of place and of our place in the world. Walking can be sociable; it can also be contemplative – gazing with love. Kim Taplin's *Walking Aloud* celebrates simply walking her patch of north Oxfordshire. She is not into great views or philosophical reflections on life; rather, she just savours, takes note of and attends to the ordinary, mundane things that she sees and the people she meets along her rambles (Taplin, 2008, p. 8). In doing so she delights in a way that St Francis would recognize.

I discovered this for myself a few years ago when undertaking the Camino, the pilgrim route across northern Spain to the shrine of St James of Compostela: 900 kilometres over the course of 40 days. It's no use for a 65-year-old carrying an 11kg backpack to attempt to hurry the journey. As well as being exposed to heat and cold, wind and rain, I became very conscious of the level of the ground beneath my feet; it seemed as if the last kilometre of the day was always uphill. Countryside can be absorbed and imprinted on the mind when you spend a whole day walking within it, and it was a wonderful way of meeting and engaging with strangers. Since the outbreak of the Covid-19 pandemic we have become used to walking and cycling for daily exercise. As the lockdown is lifted we are encouraged to continue the practice in order to reduce congestion on roads and public transport, and to keep fit and healthy. It also allows us to see into the life of the city more deeply, to pay attention to who and what is around us, and to love the place we are in.

Inhabiting

To recognize what is happening to our world requires a commitment not only to attention but to place:

> The early blooming of a particular flower, an unusually thin layer of ice on a lake, the late arrival of a migratory bird – noticing these small changes requires the kind of communion that comes from knowing a place deeply, not just as scenery but also as sustenance, and when local knowledge is passed on with a sense of sacred trust from one generation to another. (Klein, 2015, pp. 158–9)

St Francis had a great affection for the city of Assisi and its surrounding countryside. Although his preaching occasionally took him beyond central Italy, most notably to Egypt and the Holy Land in 1219–20, most of his life was spent in Umbria, 'the Green Heart of Italy', as tourist brochures describe it today. The tiny church of St Mary of the Angels in the woods some four kilometres from Assisi, which became home to his original group of brothers, held a particular place in his heart. Every year at Pentecost the growing band of brothers would gather there for an annual 'chapter' to renew fellowship with each other, to pray and to plan the missions for the year ahead. When in the last months of his life he was terminally ill, he was cared for in the palace of the Bishop of Assisi. In his final days, knowing that he was close to death, he requested that he be brought back to the Portiuncula, the 'Little Portion' as he referred to St Mary of the Angels, but not before blessing the city that had nurtured him from the cradle.

This affection for his home city was not exclusive, for he had a delight in the hermitages in the remote Umbrian countryside where he spent periods of time. It seems he had an eye for humble yet beautiful spots that became precious to him. For me, it's among the wildflowers in spring on the top of Monte Subasio overlooking the Apennine range of hills that I can sense that love of place that was so strong in Francis' life. It is affection that makes a place – and all that is in it, both human and non-human – sacred.

The American farmer, essayist and poet Wendell Berry writes of the difference between the mind of the agrarian, committed to a particular place and community, and that of an economic entrepreneur whose commitment follows wherever the money goes. In his 2012 Jefferson Lecture, entitled 'It All Turns on Affection', he spoke of his grandfather, a farmer of tobacco on a modest acreage of land on which he had laboured and which he had loved all his life. Never prosperous, suffering hardship in years of bad harvests or low prices, he made only one long journey away from the farm and its locality during his whole life:

He went with my father southward across Kentucky and into Tennessee. On their return, my father asked him what he thought of their journey. He replied: 'Well, sir, I've looked with all the eyes I've got, and I wouldn't trade the field behind my barn for every inch I've seen.'

One of the characteristics of life for many people today is that we tend to live in a number of different places over the course of our lives. I doubt that many readers of this book will be living in the city, town or village where they were born, let alone the same house. In Plaistow very many, myself included, are migrants to the area. In some schools around us one-third of the pupils move on within a school year. Around the UK generally, many face considerable commuting journeys to work, and although working from home via the internet is common, and at the time of writing mandatory, that doesn't necessarily encourage rootedness in the locality. A fallout from this transitoriness is a lack of social cohesion; it's hard to have a sense of community with your immediate neighbours if you have only just arrived in the place, if your attention is elsewhere and if your house is more of a dormitory than a home.

Brother Julian, one of those with whom I now live, has been at The House of Divine Compassion for more than 35 years. Unlike Benedictine monks and nuns who take a vow of stability to a particular monastery, Franciscans are itinerants. Over my 45 years I've lived in seven different places, including short periods in the Solomon Islands and Zimbabwe. Julian's long period in Plaistow is therefore unusual and it has given him an extraordinarily deep insight to this neighbourhood, its inhabitants and its history. More than almost anyone around here, he inhabits the place. His affection for Plaistow is tangible; it shapes the life of the house and the lives of those who find here a place of peace and sanctuary.

There's a world of difference between residing in a place and inhabiting it. The former may result in knowledge about an area: its street layout, where the shops are, where its key institutions are based. Habitation, on the other hand, requires an emotional and moral commitment to the specific, immediate place where we live: to all its inhabitants, both human and non-human. Such indwelling can open to us the recognition that the place, wherever we are, is sacred.

Valuing

Our difficulty with inhabiting the earth is caused not only by the social and geographical mobility that is common today; we live within an overarching worldview that has been shaping our Western culture for the past four centuries. The scientific method, stemming from the thinking and writing of the seventeenth-century French philosopher René Descartes, established a dualism between the 'thinking self' and the objective substance of the world around us. In his philosophy, the natural world is separate from us, an object to be explored, exploited and consumed by us. Jonathan Bate summarizes the effect of Descartes' thought:

> In the final section of his *Discourse on Method*, Descartes wrote of a practical philosophy which would enable us to know the 'power and effects of fire, water, air, the stars, the heavens and all the other bodies which surround us' – we may then put them 'to all the uses for which they are appropriate, and thereby make ourselves, as it were, masters and possessors of nature'. We will invent 'an infinity of devices by which we might enjoy, without any effort, the fruits of the earth and all its commodities.' (Bate, 2000, p. 137)

Such an approach has led to a fundamental and in many ways beneficial transformation of life for the human race but it has been at huge cost to the earth and to our relationship with it.

Understanding the material world as simply a resource to be exploited and consumed has led to a sense of alienation from it. This view can be compared to that of the Cathars, a heretical sect in the time of Francis who saw the material world as essentially unspiritual. This is a distancing from the world that involves the loss of the sense that everything has an intrinsic as well as a utilitarian value. Approaching the world as 'a giant warehouse of stuff, there for our convenience' (Williams, 2007, p. 50), has led to the ecological crisis we are now experiencing. Exploitation and exhaustion of land, water and minerals, destruction of rainforest and other habitats, collapse of biodiversity and extinction of species all follow from the idea that natural material is just 'stuff' for our use and that we stand apart from nature as its masters. It also leads to the problem of what to do with it all when we have finished exploiting and consuming it.

The opening of his conscience to the preciousness of created matter came to Dave Bookless of the Christian environmental organization, A Rocha UK, while on holiday many years ago on the island of St Martin's in the Scilly Isles. When he asked locals where to put the household waste, he was told to burn what was burnable and to take the rest to a small cove at one end of the island. Walking down the cliff path he was shocked to come across a beautiful little beach piled high with the island's rubbish. Within him he heard the Lord saying: 'How do you think I feel about what you are doing to my world?' 'It was a visceral moment', he recounts. 'I had always had an intellectual knowledge of God's delight in his creation, but this brought home to me that what was before me was symptomatic of a broken relationship with the planet, with each other and with God' (Bookless, 2010, pp. 13–16).

I've felt the same when I have found fly-tipped household and building waste on the verges of the lanes around Hilfield, or dumped on the street in Plaistow. It's often said by Christians that our culture is 'too materialist'. In fact, it is not nearly materialist enough. By seeing the material world solely in terms of its utilitarian value – how to use and consume it – we become blind to its intrinsic worth. When we have finished with it, we then dump it in places where it often becomes toxic to the ecosphere and to other humans. From the practice of casually discarding inert material it is not a far step to doing the same to our fellow humans; too many people are consigned to the waste dump of poverty, deprivation and homelessness.

At our friaries there used to be what was called the 'Jolly

Cupboard', containing clothes, usually second-hand, that had been donated to the community. Any brother could help himself on the understanding that he would in turn put into the cupboard any items he no longer needed. It was a good system because clothes tended to circulate around the community and you might recognize on someone else an article you had been wearing for years. The Jolly Cupboard has now been superseded by local charity shops which provide an even wider opportunity not just for the exchange of clothes but also for furnishing the household.

Brother Hugh, a member of the community at Hilfield Friary, is a champion recycler who expends considerable time and energy in encouraging people to sort their rubbish; he takes advantage of every opportunity to fill up a vehicle that might be passing the local recycling depot. So committed is he not only to recycling but also to reusing that he sometimes comes back with more than he went with. He is also the one who gives tender love and attention to the friary's ancient but effective sewage plant. A belief in the incarnation means caring about the drains. Living in the way of Blessed Francis, and all that flows from his life, involves the recognition that there is no essential separation between the material and the spiritual; we only know the latter through the former, however mundane and humble that may be.

Under the portico outside the church of St Martin-in-the-Fields overlooking Trafalgar Square in central London is a sculpture of a newborn baby embedded in a block of Portland stone, the same stone of which the church is built. The child is attached by its umbilical cord to the stone in which it is set. Around the sides of the block are words from the opening chapter of St John's Gospel: 'The Word was made flesh and dwelt among us' (John 1.14). The incarnation, which was so central to Francis' devotion and to the theologians who followed him, compels us to take the world and every part of it seriously. If God chooses to inhabit the material stuff of creation, then 'this created world is not simply a stage for human activity or a backdrop to human longings ... the whole of creation has meaning. It comes from God, gives glory to God and is intended to return to God' (Delio, 2003, p. 23). A Franciscan approach to creation involves a positive materialism that recognizes and values the unique 'this-ness' of every creature as pointing towards Christ. Matter matters: how we use it, how we relate to it, and how we continue to respect it once our own relationship with it has come to an end.

Gazing

I have a favourite walk at Hilfield, a circular route that takes me up the steep hill above the friary and then leads across the fields along an outcrop of the Downs. There's a certain point in the route from which one has a more than 180-degree view. At 90 degrees to the left I glimpse the top of Pilsdon Pen, the highest point in Dorset. Turning my eyes clockwise there's the faint blue outline of the Quantock Hills of Somerset. More or less straight ahead I see the lower-lying Polden Hills which hide the Somerset levels beyond them; the tor of Glastonbury is often visible with the ridge of the Mendips as a backdrop. Further round, King Alfred's Tower, built to commemorate his victory over the Danish leader Guthrum at the Battle of Eddington in 878, stands proud of the end of the Wiltshire Plain, and at 90 degrees to the right, the edge of the Dorset Downs leans in and out over the Blackmore Vale, which Thomas Hardy refers to in his novels as 'The Land of the Little Dairies'. I know the names of many of the farms around the friary and the families that farm them: I've walked the footpaths across their land. For me, it's a profoundly satisfying view of which I never tire, even on days when the clouds are low, grey and full of rain so that there's not much to see.

The sense I have when standing there is not just of myself gazing with delight at the land below, but also of myself being gazed upon with love, mercy and joy. Patrick Woodhouse, in his commentary on the words from Psalm 63, 'So would I gaze upon you in your holy place' (Woodhouse, 2015, p. 73) refers to the poet Rilke gazing from the outside which in turn leads to that which is gazed upon being imprinted within:

Through all beings the one space extends:
Outer space within.
The birds fly silently through us.
Oh, I, who would grow, I look outside, and in me grows
  the tree.
(Rilke, 2011, p. 116)

Is this what Bonaventure is referring to when he speaks of creation as a mirror, reflecting, revealing God to us? For God gazes
upon all that he has made and sees that it is very good (Gen.
1.31). Francis must have recognized that loving gaze reflected
back towards him as he walked the streets of Assisi, rejoiced
in the larks, held a cricket in his hand, and embraced a leper
on the wayside.

Of course, not everyone has a spectacular view over glorious
countryside on their doorstep. But through my rambles around
London with Bob Gilbert I have come to enjoy walking the
urban streets where I live and getting to know the 'feel' of the
area; I pay attention to the trees that line the roads and the
structure and shape of the buildings. I value the open spaces,
the small corners of green as well as wonderful parks. I even
rejoice in the weeds in the pavement! A daily walk is good
exercise, but through our senses it can also open us to what
Pope Francis calls 'the caress of God' (Francis, 2015, p. 43).

'A Walk of Thanksgiving and Praise' is a practice in which
time is spent, while walking, in deliberately paying attention
to each of the five senses in turn – sight, sound, touch, smell
and taste. By offering thanks and praise to God after savouring each sense, one can participate, like Francis and after the
pattern of Jacopone da Todi in his Lauds, in that delight that
draws us deeper into the joy and love of the Creator, Sustainer
and Giver of Life.

Questions for reflection

- What are the practices in your life that help you to pay attention to the world around you?
- How could 'reduce, reuse, recycle' help you recognize the inherent value of every part of the world?
- How does the environmental crisis and that of Covid-19 challenge or change your own view of the world?

Further reading

Brian Draper, 2012, *Less is More: Spirituality for Busy Lives*, Oxford: Lion Hudson.

Bob Gilbert, 2018, *Ghost Trees: Nature and People in a London Parish*, London: Saraband.

Michael McCarthy, 2010, *Say Goodbye to the Cuckoo*, London: John Murray.

9

Family

[Francis] would call creatures, no matter how small, by the name of 'brother' or 'sister' because he knew that they shared with him the same beginning. (II.590)

Holy obedience ... is subject and submissive to everyone in the world, not only to people but to every beast and wild animal as well. (I.165)

Understanding the fundamental interrelationship of all things, ourselves included, is the key to the reconciliation of the world. It is in letting go of possession and control, and in accepting the necessary limits of our impact on the world, that healing, peace and fullness of life for all are found.

Connectedness

One of the blessings of life at Hilfield is the bread that is provided for the refectory table. Baked in the friary kitchen, two or three times a week there's the delicious waft of loaves being taken from the oven. It's not just that the bread smells and tastes good; the loaves have character, reflecting the type of flour that has been used, the temperature of the oven that day, and the hand and personality of the baker. There are several members of the community who are involved with baking. Each has his or her own method; one uses the natural yeast in the flour to make sourdough bread, another likes to include a variety of flours, and yet another has the habit of adding left-over porridge to the dough. It's not surprising that the loaves come out different!

The bread on the table is a sign of our life together, a reminder that we are 'companions': those who eat bread together. It's a reminder, too, that we are connected, not just with each other and our guests who share the common table with us, but with people and life beyond the friary. Within every loaf of bread there's a whole chain of relationships because we know its provenance. The flour comes from Cann Mill near Sturminster Newton in Dorset. A mill on that site is mentioned in the Domesday Book. It is still powered by water and the Stoate family have been milling there for nearly 150 years. Much of the grain comes from fields within a 60 kilometre radius. We know Michael the miller and Steve who delivers the sacks of flour to us once a month. There's a similar sense of relationship with the unleavened wafers used at the daily Eucharist, made and sent to us by our Poor Clare sisters at Freeland, Oxford-shire. With this staple food we have an awareness that we live by grace and that we belong: to each other, to those who serve us, to the whole family of creation, and to the life-giving Source of all.

The sense of such connectedness was at the heart of Francis' worldview, so much so that he addressed every creature as being a 'brother' or a 'sister' within the family of creation. This may seem quaint to our contemporary understanding, but it is a fact that we have common ancestry with all that is around us: 98 per cent of our genes we share with those of an orang-utan, and more than 60 per cent with those of a banana! We are made of stardust. We are humans of the humus. In the second creation account in the Bible, the first human is known as Adam because he is made of the *adamah*, the earth (Gen. 2.15).

In Francis' language of fraternity is the recognition that we are intimately connected with every species of animal and plant, and with every atom of existence. Because of that our actions have an impact on every other creature and in turn we are dependent upon them for our life and well-being. There's irony in the fact that as the exploration of biology, chemistry and physics has expanded human knowledge of the world, the awareness of our being an integral part of the 'family of creation' has diminished so that we think and speak of 'nature' and 'the natural world' as being 'other' than us. In fact, we are as much part of the natural world as the dung beetle or the snowflake: our lives depend upon the same chemical and biological processes, and, Franciscans would add, the same love that holds us all in existence.

This lack of awareness of the connectedness of all life can be seen in our ambivalent and fractured relationship with what we eat. Food, which should be a sign of our connectedness and our dependence upon the providence of God, has become for many just fuel for the body – something to satisfy the taste buds and to keep us going to the next meal. On the one hand, we are passionate about food and rejoice in the wide variety from around the world that is offered in supermarket food halls. Television food programmes have become popular entertainment: the *Great British Bake Off* draws record audiences. Chefs are celebrities, and books about food proliferate. On the other hand, industrial agriculture and food production means that we have no knowledge of where our food comes from and little understanding of how it is grown, reared and processed. We rely upon a plentiful supply of cheap food, but most people have no idea of its true cost: not just the price paid in the shop, but also the cost in human labour and the cost to the land and environment. Having busy lives, people tend to reach for fast or convenience food; the practice of sitting around a table for a leisurely shared meal is reserved for special occasions.

It is estimated that one-third of all the food produced in the world is wasted, either on the farm, in the market or in the home. Many people suffer health problems caused by obesity, yet many experience malnutrition and hunger. It is said that the 'developed world', with its reliance on food from elsewhere, lives only seven meals away from famine. The fragility of the food chain, and of our interdependence with the rest of creation, has been demonstrated during the coronavirus crisis. Once the lockdown was announced, supermarket shelves were rapidly emptied of basic items as people feared that supplies would be interrupted. Suddenly, we became aware that it is unwise to take the food chain for granted.

David Scott's poem 'A Long Way From Bread', written for the Hilfield Friary Families' Camp, expresses the importance of recognizing our relationship with bread and of 'closing the gap' between ourselves and all things:

We have come so far from bread.
Rarely do we hear the clatter of the mill wheel;
see the flour in every cranny,
the shaking down of the sack, the chalk on the door,
the rats, the race, the pool,
baking day, and the old loaves:
cob, cottage, plaited, brick.

We have come so far from bread.
Once the crock said 'BREAD'
and the bread was what was there,
and the family's arm went deeper down each day
to find it, and the crust was favoured.

We have come so far from Bread.
Terrifying is the breach between wheat and table,
wheat and bread, bread and what goes for bread.
Loaves now come in regiments, so that loaf
is not the word. Hlaf
is one of the oldest words we have.

I go on about bread
because it was to bread
that Jesus trusted
the meaning he had of himself.
It was an honour for the bread
to be the knot in the Lord's handkerchief
reminding him about himself. So,
O bread, breakable;
O bread, given;
O bread, a blessing;
count yourself lucky bread.

Not that I am against wafers,
especially the ones produced under steam
from some hidden nunnery
with our Lord crucified into them.
They are at least unleavened, and fit the hand,
without remainder, but it is still
a long way from bread.
Better for each household to have its own bread,
daily, enough and to spare,
dough the size of a rolled towel,
for feeding angels unawares.
Then if the bread is holy,
All that has to do with bread is holy;
Board, knife, cupboard,
So that the gap between all things is closed
In our attention to the bread of the day.

I know that
'man cannot live on bread alone'.
I say, let us get the bread right.
(Scott, 2014, p. 22)

In the version of the Lord's Prayer found in the 1662 Book of Common Prayer – on which many of an older generation will have been brought up – we pray 'Thy will be done *in* earth, as it is in heaven'. Modern versions have replaced 'in' with 'on'. This small change, which may seem inconsequential, in fact represents the profound shift in approach to the world that has taken place in the past few hundred years. If we are 'on' the earth, we are also over it, signifying superiority and control. If we are 'in' the earth, then we follow the pattern of Christ who humbles himself to dwell in creation and participates in every aspect of its life.

Care

The sense of 'family membership', which attention to our staple food gives us, involves responsibility towards the other family members. In Scripture, Adam, the man of the earth, is mandated to 'till and keep' the soil (Gen. 2.15). The biblical theologian Ellen Davis points out that the Hebrew words from which this phrase is translated are *abad* and *shamar*, which also have the meaning 'to serve' and 'to preserve or guard' (Davis, 2009, pp. 29–30). The same two Hebrew words are applied to working for a landlord and to keeping the commandments. In the writings about Francis we have seen his obedience to this vocation of service towards his brothers and sisters of creation: his keen observation and gentle attention, his provision for their care and his blessing.

Some today argue that the idea of human 'stewardship' nevertheless implies a holding of power over other creatures – an anthropocentric standpoint that has led to the exploitation of the planet for the benefit of humans alone. However, Francis' 'piety' towards all, his acknowledgement of the family of creation, expresses a relationship of mutuality. The way of fraternity/sorority is to come alongside and learn from family members rather than manipulating or providing solutions for them from above.

Questions are rightly raised today about the role of genetic modification of plants and animals. The modification of genes has been going on ever since biological life began on the planet and humans have learnt the advantages of careful breeding. However, the ability to make rapid and radical adaptation to all forms of life gives us a power that needs to be used with humility and wisdom, and with a sensitivity that such changes can affect our relationship with the natural world and with each other. The fact that just a few global corporations possess the patents for most of the world's staple grains is a form of control that often disregards our essential interdependence with each other and with the rest of creation.

A tension can sometimes be perceived between caring for the endangered planet and caring for those who are poor and suffering among our fellow humans. Francis would not have understood any distinction between these two: both humans and other creatures were his brothers and sisters; and his encounter with each led him to recognize the mercy, the beauty and the love of God. As Pope Francis emphasizes, 'We are faced not with two separate crises, one environmental and the other social, but rather with one complex crisis which is both social and environmental' (Francis, 2015, p. 70). Those who are poor and disempowered in the world are the ones most likely to suffer from the pollution of land, oceans and atmosphere, and who are most vulnerable to the climate chaos that causes destruction and affects food supply.

Behind poverty, war and mass migration there is often environmental stress. The long civil war in the Democratic Republic of Congo has been fuelled by the battle for control of the precious minerals that are valued in the developed world. The conflict that has turned Syria into a war zone began following a prolonged drought, from 2007 to 2011, which caused widespread crop failure and a mass migration to urban centres. Our Franciscan brothers in the Solomon Islands speak of concessions sold to international logging companies that clear-fell the rainforest, leading to the erosion of topsoil and the loss of habitat for the species of plants and animals on which local people rely. As a result, there is a drift of young villagers into the capital, Honiara, in order to find work but they often end up in poverty. The brothers there are also concerned about the large foreign-owned trawlers that drastically reduce fish stocks, the main source of protein for many islanders. Rising sea levels threaten the viability of life on the low-lying islands from where some of the brothers come.

At Hilfield Friary, hospitality towards guests, including those who come for respite from difficult situations, goes hand in hand with working towards establishing a sustainable pattern of life and the establishment of a local conservation area to preserve the habitat for a threatened species of butterfly. The ministry of a priest who is a member of the Franciscan Third Order involves the nurture and well-being of a fragile rural community where farming no longer provides a secure income.

In London, Birmingham and Leeds brothers give sanctuary and support to people seeking asylum from countries where clean air, healthy food and a safe, peaceful and stable environment have been lacking. In each place respect for and service of the whole family of creation – both human and non-human – is a fundamental Franciscan calling.

Reconciliation

Humans have lived in close relationship with the rest of creation for 40,000 generations and it is only comparatively recently that most of us have become distanced from our natural surroundings. It is estimated that the average UK urban citizen now spends between 90 and 95 per cent of their life indoors, and therefore out of direct contact with the life of the natural world. Two things I have missed particularly on moving from Dorset to London are the sound of wind in the trees and the night sky lit with stars. In a predominantly urban and indoor culture we suffer from a wound to our psyche that has been called 'nature deficit disorder'. However, it is a wound that can be healed. A recent study has shown that hospital patients in wards with a view of countryside, or at least of trees and plants, tend to recover health more quickly than those who look out onto other buildings or a blank wall. Contact with the natural world is good for our health and well-being because it restores us to our fundamental membership of creation.

For many who come to stay at Hilfield, the opportunity to work alongside others in the kitchen, on the garden or out in the fields is a re-membering experience. People arrive at the friary tired and stressed and find refreshment and healing in digging the vegetable patch or working as part of a team laying a hedge. The Pilsdon Community, 30 kilometres to the west of Hilfield, offers longer-term rehabilitation on its smallholding of land for people struggling with addiction, mental health difficulties and social disconnection. It's wonderful what weeding a flower bed, heaving bales of hay or shovelling manure can do for you!

There are now more than a thousand projects established in the UK that operate on the basis of nature as 'co-therapist'; many of them are in cities. Sydenham Garden in south London was founded in 2002 by a group of local residents in cooperation with their GP practice with the aim of 'enabling people to improve their quality of life, social interaction and physical and mental health in a supportive community environment' (see the Sydenham Garden website, www.sydenhamgarden. org.uk). Doctors prescribe social and eco-therapy which can be more effective than medication. Closer at hand, the beautiful walled garden of our friary in Plaistow provides peace and sanctuary for local residents who come to the house: it's also a precious reconnection with Mother Earth for the brothers.

Connecting with creation can lead to the reconciliation of communities and can build bridges between people of different backgrounds and social groups. A Rocha UK's project in Southall, west London, has brought together Sikhs, Muslims and Christians in transforming a triangle of derelict land between three railway lines, previously a place for flytipping and drug abuse, into the Minet Country Park. In working for the care of 'our common home', relationships of trust and friendship have been forged.

Often it is food that creates community between people of different backgrounds, and between people and the natural environment. An organization called Migrateful runs cookery classes led by refugees, asylum seekers and migrants who are struggling to integrate and access employment. The classes provide opportunities, not just for learning English and building confidence, but also for promoting contact and cultural exchange with the wider community (see www.migrateful. org). Foodbanks, although an indictment of an economy that fails to provide an adequate means of livelihood for people on the margins of society, are also a focus for community, offering not just food but also friendship, care and encouragement.

On the wall of the refectory at Hilfield there's a whiteboard used for writing up the ingredients of the meal that is being served and where they have come from. As with the loaves, this gives an awareness of the food chain. There's a sense of satisfaction when most of the meal has had its origin in the friary's garden or fields; many of those around the table will have had a hand in its production. It is also a reminder that the friary community includes the land in which it is earthed.

Richard, the community member who for several years was responsible for the fruit and vegetable garden at the friary, speaks of 'Franciscan gardening' as learning to live with the other members of the family, including brother slug and sister greenfly. Even these two siblings, normally regarded by gardeners as major pests to be exterminated, have a role to play in the life of the family by helping to compost decaying vegetation and in being food for other more obviously beneficial creatures. So don't exterminate them with chemicals that can have a detrimental knock-on effect for other species, but first create habitats for birds, toads, hedgehogs and wasps that predate on them. Only when that fails should a more intrusive intervention be resorted to. Wise gardening involves the skill, whenever possible, of living peaceably, reconciled with the other family members.

Cattle, sheep, pigs and hens are also members of the Hilfield land community, and play their part in fertilizing the meadows, cropping the grass and wildflowers and providing delicious meat for the refectory. Some express surprise that as Franciscans we lovingly husband animals and then send them to be slaughtered for food. There's certainly a case today for vegetarianism or veganism. Industrial-scale livestock farming prevents us from recognizing the true cost of meat: the life of the animal that has been taken, and the huge input of natural resources that has been necessary to bring it to the supermarket shelf at a competitive price. However, there's no evidence that Francis himself refrained from eating meat: the brothers were told to 'eat what is set before them' – though, living among the poorest in the community, meat would have been an occasional feast rather than part of a regular diet. Butchering a carcass at the friary involves respect and thanksgiving for the life of the animal, and a care not to waste any part of it – offal is often on the menu – so that each meal is a celebration of the gift of life received for that day.

Recognition of the interdependence of human life and the natural world is less obvious in the heart of the city, but I have encountered plenty of encouraging signs since moving to London. There are urban farms at Spitalfields, on the Isle of Dogs and in Newham. There are allotments, and long queues for one becoming available. Close by to us on the Greenway, which runs along the bank over the East London Sewage Outfall, a community orchard has been planted. In the neighbouring borough of Tower Hamlets, home to a large Bengali-speaking population, many of the courtyards between the blocks of flats contain raised beds for the growing of beans, gourds and pumpkins. These are enclosed with wire caging to prevent vandalism. The produce is available at one or other of the local shops, but to have these home-grown is as much a part of the culture of Bangladeshis as is the garden-produced tomatoes for an Italian family. This summer I have followed their example and dug up part of the lawn in our garden to create raised beds for runner beans and spinach. Even a balcony or window-sill can become a sacramental place: of creation reconciled, redeemed and renewed.

Bonaventure warns of the danger of finding ourselves 'at war' with the rest of creation:

> Open your eyes, alert the ears of your spirit, open your lips and apply your heart so that in all creatures you may see, hear, praise, love and worship, glorify and honour your God, lest the whole world rise up against you ... For because of this the whole world will fight against the foolish. (Bonaventure, 1978, p. 67)

In the two crises we are facing, of climate change and the coronavirus, with language being used of 'battling wildfires' and the 'hidden enemy' of Covid-19, it feels as though war has already begun. The Franciscan tradition speaks to us instead of the path of reconciliation. The perception of being part of the whole family of creation points a way to the healing of the gaping wound in our planet caused by our forgetfulness of the interconnection of life under the loving and sustaining gaze of

God. Rediscovering our membership of the family is a major step on the way to reconciliation with the rest of creation and the repair of our common home threatened with ruin.

Minority

The chapel at the friary in Plaistow, dedicated to the Divine Compassion, is an unprepossessing place, housed in a prefabricated chalet erected as a temporary structure back in 1970. However, looking out onto the garden, it's a local version of the tiny church of St Mary of the Angels in the woods below Assisi, which became for Francis and his first brothers their much-loved place of prayer and worship. Here, most mornings of the week, the Eucharist is celebrated to renew our participation in the life of the Son of God who 'hides himself under an ordinary piece of bread'. It was this humble self-emptying of God in the Eucharist that amazed Francis, and he saw it in every aspect of the life of Jesus from the crib to the cross. It shaped his self-understanding and it directed his approach to all that was around him.

On account of this humility of God, Francis called himself and his brothers *Fratres Minores* or Lesser Brothers. He wanted to follow in the footsteps of the One who, forsaking his high throne in heaven, had become 'lesser' in order to be alongside us as our brother. There was an additional significance in the title for him because, as the son of the wealthy up-and-coming merchant Pietro di Bernadone, he had in his youth sought to rise to the rank of a knight and to be honoured among the *majores* or the 'big people', the land-owning class of the city. Identifying himself and his brothers as '*minores*' was a deliberate act of self-emptying.

On the edge of the City of London a street named Minories runs north from the Tower of London to Aldgate. It is so called because it was where the Poor Clare sisters, also known as the Minoresses, established a convent soon after arriving in England in the first half of the thirteenth century. The street at that time ran just outside the eastern city wall, which had been a line of defence and demarcation since Roman times. The convent has long gone, dissolved at the Reformation by Henry VIII, and the street is now lined with towering office blocks, part of one of the great financial centres of the world where currencies are traded by the millions and large salaries are earned. The name, however, lingers and points to a characteristic of the early Franciscans, both brothers and sisters, who chose to live in situations outside the security of city walls where the poorest people dwelt without the privileges of citizenship.

The vocation of Franciscans is to respond to the one who out of love has become 'lesser' for us by meeting and serving 'the poor Christ' in the lives of those on the margins of society. To do so involves the choice to embrace 'minority'. Francis and his original band of brothers were drawn by divine compassion to be among those who suffered with leprosy. The friars who arrived in Cambridge in the year 1225 joyfully accepted accommodation among prisoners in the town lock-up because that was where they expected to meet their incarnate Lord. Anglican Franciscans came onto the scene comparatively late in the story, but as with their predecessors it was the humble self-emptying of God in Jesus that inspired and motivated them. The Society of Divine Compassion, founded by a group of four Anglicans in 1894 in Plaistow – at that time an area of poor housing and great social need – was committed to live at the same standard of living as those around them; likewise the sisters of the Community of St Francis, first in Hull and then in Dalston, east London.

For the small group of 'brown brothers' who founded The Home of St Francis at Flowers Farm in Dorset in the early 1920s, it was the large number of destitute men tramping the roads looking for work in the aftermath of World War One, that led them to follow Francis' way of minority. Brother Douglas, the leader of that community, was deeply concerned about the harsh and unhealthy conditions in the 'casual wards' which at that time were the only provision for 'men-of-the-road'. Like Francis, his character combined determination and humility and his approach was to share something of the deprivation and humiliation of those trapped in a pattern of vagrancy. He and those with him lived simply with the 'wayfaring brothers' who found their way to the friary for respite or rehabilitation. The brothers worked alongside them on the land and would visit and stay in casual wards in order to meet inmates, to show solidarity with them and to learn at first hand about their needs and the issues of vagrancy at that time. In such a way they came to know and serve the Christ who tramped the roads of England between the two world wars (Dunstan, 1997, pp. 46ff.).

Francis told his brothers to 'be subject to every beast and wild animal' (I.165) and in his Canticle of the Creatures he sang of 'our sister, Mother Earth, who sustains and governs us'. The idea of being subject to the natural world and governed by it is far from the attitude of mastery and exploitation that shapes our present worldview, but it is essential for the survival of life on the planet. Any wise farmer or gardener will say that the most important skill is to pay attention and be obedient to the ten inches of topsoil that lies over the surface of the land. Knowing its particular gifts, qualities and characteristics and preserving its fertility are essential to producing good crops.

I discovered this for myself in my early days at Hilfield, when I decided to dig over a corner of one of the fields to plant brassicas. 'They won't do anything there,' said Brother Anselm, who had worked in the friary garden 30 years previously, 'nothing ever grows there'. True to his words, the cabbages failed: I should have listened to his advice. The beautiful word 'husbandry' involves humility, the acceptance of limits and the recognition that the land knows best.

Being subject to every creature includes not just farming and gardening but all aspects of life. A first-time visitor to one of our friaries often expresses surprise that it doesn't look like a monastery. Neither the friary at Hilfield, nor that in Plaistow, nor Glasshampton Monastery, were built for that purpose, but have been converted from other uses. Hilfield was a farmhouse surrounded by barns and cottages which became, for a short time in the early years of the last century, a school known as The Little Commonwealth. Although a couple of buildings were added by the brothers in the 1960s, the others are in the local vernacular building style of flint and brick; one of them is a typical Dorset thatched cottage. The House of Divine Compassion in Plaistow dates back to the eighteenth century when it was possibly a Master Mariner's house. Today it is wedged between a redundant leisure centre on one side and flats on the other. Without the sign 'Helping Hands' over the door and the tau cross, much loved by Francis, you wouldn't know from the outside that Franciscans live there. There's a Franciscan minority about both of these places and about our other friaries around the world.

Limits

'Lesser' involves accepting limits; looking for what is at hand rather than running after the latest advertised innovation. It means eating seasonally rather than buying food flown in from other parts of the world. It means understanding and respecting the living story of a place and its people rather than being insulated from it in one's own world. It involves discovering the names of people and creatures, both animate and inanimate, and in that way establishing a relationship with them. Hilfield's focus on the care of creation has been about this kind of subjection. The friary heating and hot water supply has been converted to run on wood harvested from our own and neighbouring land, and red cedar from the same woodland has been used to make benches for the chapel. Solar-voltaic cells generate some of the friary's electricity, which in turn powers an electric car for local journeys. The Dorset style of hedge-laying has been learnt and the friary has reverted to long-established custom at Passiontide of using the goat willow, with its golden catkins flowering in early spring, for the Palm Sunday procession. Field names have been chosen or recovered from a nineteenth-century tithe map.

The recognition of limit holds an important economic wisdom for our times. One of the reasons that Francis strictly forbade his brothers even to touch money was because:

In line with the economic ideas of his time he was convinced that the quantity of money available in the world was constant and that by enriching oneself and especially in storing up coinage – but also in stocking foodstuffs, as merchants were then doing, while waiting to be able to sell them at the best price – one was depriving others of such things. (Vauchez, 2012, p. 108)

In the liberal economic thinking that governs the world today, the fact that the money supply is bounded by nothing except the credit-worthiness of those who create it has led to the illusion that there can be no limit to economic growth and the exploitation of the resources of the planet.

The ordering of the economic and political life of the world has been based for many years upon the assumption that the gross domestic product (GDP) of nations and of the world is the fundamental measure of human well-being; also on the idea that growth of GDP is both beneficial to all and has no limit. A report by Christian Aid questions this 'unexamined good' (Christian Aid, 2017, p. 9). While acknowledging that some economic growth is necessary, in particular for developing nations that are seeking to raise their citizens out of poverty, it challenges the theory that the poor always benefit from the increase of general wealth that is supposed to 'trickle down' to them. Development and control of resources in these countries by global corporations often leads to disempowerment for those at the bottom of the ladder, the destruction of local communities, and a widening of the gap between rich and poor.

Plaistow, which is sandwiched between the tower blocks of Canary Wharf, housing the offices of international banks, and the development of Stratford City, which is marketed as 'the hip place in London to live', demonstrates this gap. Although many new apartments are being built, most of them are well beyond the price range of those in the area who live on or below the minimum wage. Lack of available housing that is genuinely affordable for local people is one of the major issues in this part of London. On average, 40 to 50 people a day come to our door for food.

In richer nations, especially, the market feeds a thirst for consumer goods which fills a void of meaning in people's lives. The priority of economic growth above all else destroys eco-systems, disregards the limits of natural resources on the planet and is a major reason behind the climate crisis we are fac-ing. The Christian Aid report goes on to suggest measures of well-being for human society as alternatives to the growth of GDP: sustainability of both human and non-human life, regard for human rights, and an equality of opportunity for human flourishing. Similarly, the economist Kate Raworth argues that the economy of nations and of the world as a whole should be bounded by two fundamental constraints: the needs of the poorest in society and the load that the planet can bear (Raworth, 2018, p. 11).

It is forecast that the immediate effect of the global pandemic will be a very substantial knock to the world economy. Living in the midst of the crisis, it's hard to see what this will lead to in the longer term, but there are important lessons to be learned and economists are already reflecting upon them. Mark Carney, the former Governor of the Bank of England, points out:

In this crisis, we know we need to act as an interdependent community not independent individuals, so the values of eco-nomic dynamism and efficiency have been joined by those of solidarity, fairness, responsibility and compassion ... The great test of whether this new hierarchy of values will prevail is climate change. After all, climate change is an issue that (i) involves the entire world, from which no one will be able to self-isolate; (ii) is predicted by science to be the central risk tomorrow; and (iii) we can only address if we act in advance and in solidarity. (Carney, 2020)

Dispossession

We are blessed in the friary at Plaistow by an abundant supply of food. Each afternoon, someone from the house takes a trol-ley down the road to pick up fruit and vegetables that Jimmy, the greengrocer, gives to us because they are not quite up to standard for sale. Each evening there's a collection from food outlets in Stratford's Westfield Centre, and others regularly bring gifts of food to us. We live out of the generosity of others and share with others much of what we have been given. In the time of lockdown when there was particular need, we had daily deliveries of rice and curry from a local gurdwara.

It's easy to confuse Francis' insistence on 'holy poverty' with an anxious and life-denying asceticism, the belief that the harsher one's life is the more holy one will become. There have been endless disputes among Franciscans over the centuries about how poor they ought to be, and sometimes even a competitiveness about which particular friar or community is living the poorest! This misses the point of what Francis' betrothal to 'Lady Poverty' was about. As with his relationship with every creature, his focus was always on the one who 'though he was rich, yet for your sakes he became poor, so that through his poverty you might become rich' (2 Cor. 8.9).

Poverty for Francis was the acknowledgement and acceptance of our existential situation before God; that we have nothing but that which has been given to us by God. Following Jesus' story of the man who built bigger barns to store his bumper harvest, Francis' preaching often warned people of the danger of relying on their possessions for security. The great danger of 'riches' of any kind – money, goods and houses, but also of status, learning or class – is that they can conceal from us the fact that we are always the beneficiaries of God's abundant generosity: that we live in his economy of gift.

Our possessions can both blind us to our own essential poverty and prevent us from seeing riches in the 'other' who is poor. This is often so in a society that is unaware of, or chooses to ignore, the giftedness of those who are excluded from society by their poverty, whether that be material, social or intellectual. Francis' encounter with the leper at the beginning of his vocation was a revelation to him, not of the wealth that he, a rich young man, could bestow on a poor beggar, but of the riches of Christ, and of his fraternity with the leper. In the same way, the call to 'live lightly' on the planet is not just for some slight adjustment of lifestyle so that one can continue at the standard of living one is accustomed to. Simplicity of living arises from the recognition that the created world of which we are a part is sacred; a precious gift, revealing to us the beauty and love of its Creator and Redeemer, and which needs our self-emptying in order to flourish.

Such an economy of gift is counter-cultural to a society driven by the economy of the market, where everything has a price set against it and in which there is always competition for possession that advantages the wealthiest. As Francis saw it, to live in God's gift economy involves dispossession – the acknowledgement that we don't hold anything by right or in perpetuity because, ultimately, everything belongs to creation's giver rather than to the receiver. This is spelt out today in Catholic social teaching. Although recognizing the individual right to private property, the Church teaches that 'the goods of creation are destined for humankind as a whole' (Catechism, 2403). The Protestant reformer William Tyndale put it even more starkly back in the early sixteenth century: 'This term, "myself", is not in the gospels', and 'If ... thou yet have superfluity [of goods] and hearest necessity to be among your brethren a thousand miles off, to them art thou debtor; yea to the very infidels we be debtors if they need' (Tyndale, 1848, pp. 98–9). Franciscan simplicity of living is both a receiving and sharing of abundant gift.

Franciscan poverty is not just about the dispossession of money and property, but about the letting go of power. Francis forbade his brothers to accept privileges from the Church or to hold offices of authority in households. Those who served the Order of Friars Minor in positions of responsibility were not to be called 'abbot' or 'superior' or 'prior', titles used in monastic orders, but to hold the positions of 'Minister' and 'Custos' or 'Guardian'. It's a 'flat' form of leadership, which we try to exercise today. Once, when I was Guardian at Hilfield, I drove to the station a guest who had been staying with us for the past week. He told me that he had enjoyed his visit very much and that it seemed that everyone played a part in the life of the community. 'But,' he said, 'I couldn't work out who was in charge.' I didn't feel it necessary to enlighten him. The same kind of authority should be exercised in the care for creation as whole: non-possessive and participatory.

Hospitality

The vows of poverty, chastity and obedience, which Franciscan brothers and sisters take after a three-year novitiate period, are all of them – not just the vow of poverty – about dispossession, the surrendering of territory, in order to make room for the 'other'. The same is true, of course, for the vows of marriage. Such 'hospitality' is at the heart of that 'creation out of love' of which the Franciscan medieval theologians speak. God is a hospitable communion of love who makes room for that which is not God, in order to love that which is 'other' and to receive love in return. The Latin word *hospes* means both 'host' and 'guest' and it is in both these senses that we encounter God in the world.

All our Franciscan houses provide hospitality to guests. At Hilfield, Glasshampton and Alnmouth people come for short periods of retreat, rest and refreshment. In our urban houses in London, Birmingham and Leeds we have staying with us people who would otherwise be homeless; many of them are refugees or are applying for refugee status. In our friaries we see ourselves not as running a hotel or a hostel, but making room for people in our homes and in our lives. In south London, a member of our Franciscan Third Order welcomes a number of people to share her large house. In all these places God's gift of hospitality is being shared.

The same 'making room for the other' is involved in the care of creation. Brother Tom and I had a discussion about the garden here at Plaistow. I am more of an intensive gardener than he is, wanting to use every available space for vegetables and for cultivated flowers, whereas he urges me to leave parts of the garden wild as habitat for other creatures. We came to a compromise. I think he is more a Franciscan gardener than I am. Francis' instruction to leave the margins of the garden undisturbed for the wildflowers in order that they might give praise to God wasn't exactly a conservation project, but it was nevertheless wise ecology.

The wildflowers have spread over the meadows at Hilfield because we have sown them with yellow rattle, which is parasitic on grass. This diminishes the grass cover and so makes room for the orchids and other plants to flourish. The High Stoy Conservation Cluster is based at the friary and includes neighbouring landowners. One of its projects is to reintroduce the Duke of Burgundy to the area. Despite its rather grand title this is a small brown member of the butterfly family that is now rarely seen and is under threat. The project involves clearing the bramble and thorn scrub that has grown on the edge of the Downs to make space for the cowslips that provide the Duke's favourite food.

Within a month of the coronavirus lockdown, which prevented huge cruise liners entering, dolphins were seen playing in the Venice lagoon for the first time in decades, and species of fish returned to the canals. The speed of their reappearance seemed to express a longing. In the same period Londoners have experienced greatly improved air quality as a result of the reduction of emissions from road vehicles and airplanes. The rapid return of a wide spread of species of plant and animal, including the turtle dove which had nearly become extinct in the UK, to the Knepp Estate in Sussex since a rewilding project was established there in 2002, is another example of how the natural world can flourish if we offer it hospitality.

Francis' ultimate hospitality was to welcome 'Sister Death'. He had set out on the evangelical way by dramatically stripping himself naked before the Bishop of Assisi when his father demanded repayment of the value of the cloth that his son had taken from the warehouse to pay for the cost of materials for repairing the derelict church of San Damiano. At the end of his life, when he had been brought home to die at the friary at St Mary of the Angels, he asked his brothers to lay him naked on the ground so that he might be reconciled with death at the place he counted as his home.

The Covid-19 pandemic has brought home to us the words

from Genesis used in the liturgy of Ash Wednesday: 'Remember you are dust and to dust you shall return' (*Common Worship: Times and Seasons*, 2006, p. 230). There have been desperately sad stories of people dying from the virus, mainly those who were elderly or were already suffering from chronic illness, but also some who were young, fit and active. At the time of writing Newham has the highest ratio of deaths per head of population of any borough in the country. We have been shocked by the substantial number of nurses, doctors and care workers who have died. Bus and taxi drivers here in London have been hit hard by the disease. We have grown used over the past 75 years to keeping death at arm's length, but it is pressing in upon us in this crisis. Serious illness is often spoken of as a battle to be fought against, but in face of this virus people feel powerless.

All these feelings can and have affected us as Franciscan brothers and sisters. We have among us those who are particularly vulnerable to the disease and we recognize that any of us could succumb to it.

Following in the steps of Francis, who accepted 'our Sister Death' as part of his extended family in the Canticle of the Creatures (Moloney, 2013, p. 101), there's a particular witness to welcome this relative as a companion on our journey. We seek to prepare ourselves to give hospitality to her as a normal and expected part of our own family story. Brothers and sisters are encouraged to write a 'living will', outlining their wishes should they become seriously ill, and their preferred arrangements for their funeral. We aim to surround each other in prayer as Sister Death approaches and, whenever possible, to be alongside them physically at the time of death. Over the years I have had the privilege of watching and waiting by the bedside of a number of brothers in their last hours. I am always profoundly moved by the experience.

For Brother Kentigern, who died at a relatively early age from cancer, it was important for him and for us that we accompanied him closely in the final weeks of his life. A basket coffin was woven before he died by one of the members of the Hilfield Community. When the time came to bring his body home, a car was sent so that he wasn't borne by strangers. His grave was dug in the friary cemetery, and as the coffin was lowered into the ground we gathered around to sing Francis' Canticle, which includes the words: 'Through Death our Sister praised be from whom no-one alive can flee' (*The Daily Office SSF*, 2010, p. 532). The funeral requiem was not complete until all had taken a hand in 'filling in'. It seemed right that 'our sister, Mother Earth' should have the last line of the song.

Questions for reflection

* How can the food you eat become a sacrament of your relationship with others, with every creature and with God?
* What are the connections you can see between the climate crisis and the needs of those on the margins?
* What are the areas in your own life that you find hardest to let go of?

Further reading

Kate Raworth, 2018, *Doughnut Economics: Seven Ways to Think Like a 21st-Century Economist*, London: Random House.

Justin Welby, 2016, *Dethroning Mamon: Making Money Serve Grace*, London: Bloomsbury.

Norman Wirzba, 2018, *Food and Faith: A Theology of Eating*, Cambridge: Cambridge University Press.

IO

Song

The Lord gave me, Brother Francis, thus to begin doing penance. (I.124)

Sometimes [Francis] used to do this: a sweet melody of the spirit bubbling up inside him would become on the outside a French tune; the thread of a divine whisper which his ears heard secretly would break out in a French song. (II.142)

In this chapter we move from an awareness of our responsibility for the brokenness and fragility of the world to the joyful song of praise at the heart of creation in which we lose ourselves in 'the love that moves the sun and other stars' (Dante, 2006, p. 482).

Tears

The botanist and former Director of Kew, Sir Ghillean Prance, a friend and neighbour of ours in west Dorset who has led a number of study weekends at the friary, has spent a lifetime studying the life of plants in the Amazonian region. Over more than 40 visits he has watched with huge concern and sadness the steady destruction of that rich and very sensitive ecosystem which, besides being a major carbon sink, holds a large proportion of the world's flora and fauna. A good part of it is as yet undiscovered. He carries a deep sense of frustration and even agony that despite the overwhelming opposition of naturalists, politicians and environmental groups from around the world the clear-felling of the rainforest has continued. He has also seen how the seductive lure of money and consumer goods can be a corrupting influence with the indigenous tribes – the guardians of the forest for thousands of years – to make way for cattle and the cultivation of soya. For a time in the last decade it seemed that an agreement had been established with the Brazilian government to limit the intrusion of developers, but since the election of a new President in 2019 that has been set aside and the forest has been burning out of control. With the direct experience of such loss and destruction Sir Ghillean joins 'creation's groaning' (Rom. 8.22).

At the hermitage of Greccio in the Rieti Valley to the south of Assisi there is a picture of Francis holding a cloth to his eyes. Some believe that this is a representation of him when he was suffering from the eye disease that afflicted him in his final years and led eventually to his blindness. However, it may well be that this is simply a picture of him weeping. We remember Francis for his joy and exuberance – in creation and in the love of God. But there are many references in the sources to him in tears. The story in which he comes across two sticks on the path and takes them up to play as a viol and to sing and dance for the love of God in Jesus ends in tears as he weeps for the cost of that love on the cross (II.142). Animals, especially those that were weak and vulnerable, led him to sadness and compassion; they reminded him of the vulnerability and poverty of Christ and his mother. Bonaventure writes that he was always weeping for his own sins (II.749).

Tears played an important part in the lives of the early monks of the desert and were regarded by them as a spiritual gift. 'Let us weep,' Abba Macarius counselled his disciples, 'and let tears gush out of our eyes' (Ward, 1975, p. 136). Anthony, the father of desert monasticism, exhorted those who wished to follow the monastic path 'to weep and groan in your heart' (Ward, 1975, p. 8). The Greek word *penthos* signifies compunction, a piercing of the heart that is necessary for liberation from the sins of self-centredness, pride and despair, and that can reconnect us to the grace and mercy that flow from the source of life. Tears open the way to life with God and with each other (Christie, 2012, pp. 70ff.).

Many of the Psalms are songs of lament: for an awareness

of sinfulness, for a sense of isolation among enemies and for the absence of God, and for the experience of exile in a foreign land. Likewise, Job complains to God over his desolation. Above all, the prophet Jeremiah, in a vision of environmental catastrophe to match anything that we see today, grieves for the land of Israel, ruined on account of the people's foolishness and faithlessness:

> I looked on the earth, and lo, it was waste and void;
> and to the heavens, and they had no light.
> I looked on the mountains, and lo, they were quaking,
> and all the hills moved to and fro.
> I looked, and lo, there was no one at all,
> and all the birds of the air had fled.
> I looked, and lo, the fruitful land was a desert,
> and all its cities were laid in ruins. (Jer. 4.23–26)

Overwhelming evidence has been given by scientists of the effect on world temperature of burning fossil fuels. The link between the industrial, economic and social developments of the past 200 years and the melting ice cap, the rising sea level, the increased frequency and severity of droughts and storms, and the rapid extinction of species has been clearly shown to us. Yet there are people, including leaders of some of the world's most powerful nations and corporations, who either deny that it is happening or refuse to accept that it has anything to do with human activity. For others, the issue is just too big to deal with; they feel overwhelmed by the vast scale of the problem. Climate change denial shows that facts alone don't alter people's attitude or behaviour. It takes the breaking open of the heart to do that.

The world was deeply shocked by the image of the body of three-year-old Alan Kurdi, washed up on the coast of Turkey in September 2015 following a failed attempt by his refugee family to reach the Greek island of Kos. I was moved to tears on a visit to the cathedral at Syracuse in Sicily by a Lampedusa Cross, made from the spars of a vessel that sank when crossing with refugees from north Africa. One of those with us here in our friary in Plaistow spent several months in the Sangat refugee camp in Calais and crossed the Channel underneath a lorry, clinging to its chassis. He has waited four years so far for an appeal to remain in the UK to be heard by a court. His story has profoundly affected my understanding. Similarly, it's the sight of seabirds smothered in black crude oil, of dolphins entangled in netting and of land laid waste by the extraction of oil from tar sands in Alberta, that begins to pierce and transform people's worldview.

The closer we get to people and creatures that are suffering, the more likely we are to recognize our own involvement in their situation. For we are all complicit in the injustice and loss around us, probably not deliberately, but simply by belonging to an economic and political system heavily structured in our favour. Almost all who read this book will have benefited from the affluent lifestyle to which we have become accustomed, but for which those who are poor, and the planet itself, have borne the brunt of the cost in disadvantage, degradation and destruction. We should look into the mirror and ask ourselves: 'How do I reflect the world's thirst for oil or the greed that is destroying the planet?' (Chryssavgis, 2019, p. 124). Tears of lament can release us from imprisonment in our self-enclosed worldview and set us upon the journey home from our long exile in a foreign land, alienated from our brothers and sisters in the rest of creation.

Penance

In his *Testament*, written shortly before he died, Francis recounts that the meeting with a leper on the road outside Assisi was the beginning of his 'doing penance'. We tend to think of 'penance' as punishment, and the associated words 'repentance' and 'penitence' as feeling sorry or guilty, but the biblical word *metanoia* means 'turning around', 'facing the opposite direction'. Francis was turned around, converted, by the leper and he continued in penance/conversion for the rest of his life. 'Doing penance', for Francis, was not so much the action of putting his arms around the leper as it was the embracing of a transformed way of seeing and frame of mind that shaped his life and actions thereafter. He and his followers were sometimes called 'Brothers of Penitence'.

We are called to a lifetime of change – beginning with ourselves. We may be enthusiastic about this to start with, but the enthusiasm can soon wear off. C. S. Lewis was supposed to have said, 'Every morning when I get up I give my life to God, but I haven't finished shaving before I have taken half of it back again.' I remember a conversation in the 1970s with a young white South African Anglican priest who was campaigning for the end of apartheid. He spoke of his frustration about the attitude of many liberally minded white people in his congregation: 'They all believe in change, as long as it doesn't make any difference.' Tears of lament, rather than keeping us stuck in a sense of guilt, shame and good intention, lead to a commitment to ongoing action for change.

Eco-penitence – the recognition of the need for change that reconciles us with the rest of creation – has shaped the transformation that has happened at Hilfield over the past 15 years. The installation of the biomass heating system in 2014 involved not only the commitment of a substantial amount of capital, but also a huge amount of work by the community. In order to save on cost, we undertook to dig the 1.5 metre trenches that would accommodate the bulky insulated pipes connecting the new wood-chip boiler to the eight separate buildings of the friary. The task took nearly four months. When it began in the summer it hadn't seemed too great a challenge, but as the autumn rains began the place came to look like a World War One battlefield: there was mud everywhere. Similarly, the purchase of two neighbouring fields in 2016 has very heavily depleted the Development Fund of our SSF Province and has committed those living at Hilfield to a long programme of land and habitat restoration. Other houses of brothers and sisters here in the UK have followed Hilfield's example by insulating buildings, switching to renewable sources for electricity, and seeking other ways to reduce their carbon footprint. The turnaround continues.

The transformation to a more sane and sustainable way of

life is not just to do with the buildings and lifestyle of individuals, important though that is: it requires a change of heart and practice by governments, institutions and corporations. Experience shows that structural change comes only through using every means of representation available: contacting Members of Parliament, attending election hustings, joining campaigning organizations and signing up to petitions. Both the First and Third Orders of SSF are committed to working for justice, peace and the integrity of creation. Sometimes, direct action involving peaceful protest is not only appropriate but necessary. Several brothers and sisters, and many members of the Franciscan Third Order, took part in the gatherings of Extinction Rebellion in London and other cities in 2019, for a time occupying one of the bridges across the Thames.

Radical action is urgent, but it need not be an anxious or a gloomy business. Francis' turning towards the leper brought 'sweetness of soul and body' in place of the bitterness that the sight of lepers had previously been for him (I.124). There has been delight and playfulness for the community at Hilfield in the deeper engagement with the natural environment and in the movement to a more sustainable pattern of living. The Extinction Rebellion rallies were fun for those who took part, though perhaps not so much for those held up in traffic jams. Slowing down to pay attention, rediscovering interdependence and making room for the 'other' all lead to a fuller, more spacious and more joyful life.

Francis' question to Clare and Sylvester about whether to preach or whether to withdraw to a life of prayer and solitude received the answer that he should continue with the proclamation of the good news. Francis' action always issued from the intimacy of his life with God, which was renewed in extensive periods of prayer. This balance of prayer and action is important today. Glasshampton, our monastic house of withdrawal and silence, is a 'desert place' for us and for those who come for retreat, but contemplative practice is also essential within the busyness and distractedness of life in the city.

There is a continual danger, for Franciscans as much as for others, of becoming so engrossed in well-intentioned and gospel-inspired action that the rootedness of our life in God is lost. Our preoccupation with environmental projects and social action can divert our attention from the sacramental significance of every creature pointing towards the One who holds all things in being. We need the practice of contemplation in order to de-centre our action and renew our vision. In the 'self-forgetting gazing towards the light of God in Christ we learn how to look at one another and at the whole of God's creation'. Such gazing 'is a deeply revolutionary matter' (Williams, 2012).

Harmony

At the entrance to Hilfield Friary there is a large bell mounted on a wooden gantry. Cast at least 500 years ago, it comes from a now redundant church and is on long loan from the Diocese of Salisbury. It was placed on its present site to mark the seventy-fifth anniversary of the arrival of the first three brothers at Flowers Farm on 17 December 1921. The bell calls the community and its guests to worship in the chapel which was once the farm's cow-byre. Echoing from the hill above the friary, it booms out across the countryside below us so that on a still day it can be heard well over a mile away.

Four times a day, in answer to the bell, the brothers at Hilfield stop whatever they are doing to enter the chapel – the beating heart of the community – for the Daily Office of psalms, readings and prayer, which Nobby Clark, a wayfarer who lived with us in the 1970s and 1980s, irreverently used to call 'God-bothering'. I am unsure as to whether our sometimes croaking voices or sleepy, distracted responses disturb God, but the worship in chapel frames our daily life. The same pattern of prayer and praise takes place in all our houses and everywhere a brother or sister happens to be. I find having the psalms and readings on a smartphone useful for when I'm travelling. At the beginning of one of the services it is the custom in our houses to pray the prayer Francis wrote for when brothers should come across a church:

We adore you, Most Holy Lord Jesus Christ,
here and in all your churches throughout the world.
And we bless you
because by your holy cross
You have redeemed the world. (II.551)

For Francis, even the entering of a church building was an act of worship, bringing him to a place where he was connected to the story of God with his people that culminates in the life, death and resurrection of Jesus Christ and the outpouring of the Spirit. The rehearsing of that story day by day in reading, reciting and singing the words of the Scriptures tunes us to its cadences. We are caught up in the searching, longing, groaning, forgetting, repenting, struggling and rejoicing of God's people and God's creation. We also hear, see and feel God's patient-calling, sometimes-groaning, long-time-suffering, ever-forgiving and always-transforming love towards us. In the Daily Office and in the celebration of the Eucharist our lives are shaped for telling, singing and being part of God's story in the world.

Jonathan, who is the builder and maintenance person among the community at Hilfield, is one of the priests who presides regularly at the daily Eucharist. He often enters the chapel dressed in the eucharistic vestments but wearing boots that are covered with dust and paint from his work. Those boots are a sign to us that the service of prayer and praise in the chapel is closely connected with the work that happens outside: on the land, in the kitchen and refectory, in the welcome of guests and in serving each other and those in need. All these are part of our worship: an offering of love and a sharing in creation's praise. The word 'liturgy', which is often used as a cover-all term for a service in church, originally meant 'the work of the people'.

Haymaking is a communal task each year at Hilfield, usually in the first or second week of July after the seeds of the wild-flowers have set. This involves mowing the meadows, turning and raking the hay as it dries, and then following the baler to collect it. It is then loaded and taken to the barn for storing as winter fodder for the friary's sheep and cattle. Everyone takes part in one way or another: some are out in the field, some are in the barn, some bring refreshment, others are in the kitchen to prepare a substantial evening meal, and yet others offer prayer that the fine weather holds. It is often done under pressure to get it completed before rain spoils the crop. It can be heavy and demanding manual work, and yet there's a joy in it: for a few days the community loses itself in this 'liturgy'.

There are other more frequent friary customs that have the character of worship. The mid-morning tea-break in the court-yard, whatever the weather, has been happening since the days of Brother Douglas and the early friars. Even when it's chucking down with rain, people huddle under the cloister to greet each other, to chat, joke and share a story. The Rogation Procession in May wends its way around the land to ask blessing not just upon the crops and livestock but on every part of the friary's life and work, and to acknowledge the connection between these and the song of creation that Francis heard and sang.

I remember a *Songs of Praise* broadcast from Windsor Castle, following its restoration after the fire in 1992. One of those interviewed was a carpenter who had worked on the roof. He spoke of his joy and privilege to have had the opportunity of being part of the team of skilled craftspeople and to have been able to work on that building with the wonderful material of green oak from Windsor Park. When asked about his hymn of choice, he replied that the roof itself should be his song of praise.

Today, as I write at my Plaistow desk in early May, is the annual 'Dawn Chorus Day', designated as such by the Royal Society for the Protection of Birds because this late spring period is when birds here in the UK are at their peak of calling for mates and guarding their territories. It involved being up and out by 4.30 a.m. to hear the start of it, the blackbird in this urban garden striking the first note. This lockdown year the chorus has been especially rich because the birds have not had to compete with the first plane of the day making its approach to London Heathrow. However, it's not just the birds that we need to be attuned to; it's the whole symphony of life on the planet that we are part of.

In the daily lives of many it can be difficult to hear and join in this song. In our fragmented world, work, home, recreation and worship are often discrete, disconnected and competing activities. Maybe this is why church attendance has dropped so drastically in recent decades; there just isn't enough time to fit everything in. Yet the essential interconnectedness of our lives can still be recognized. In the Covid-19 pandemic we have become acutely aware that doctors, nurses and all health and care workers have not just been doing a job, earning a living, but have been risking and in some cases surrendering their lives for the sake of the community. A friend of mine who rarely crosses the threshold of a church remarked to me that the weekly Thursday evening applause in thanksgiving for these people was for him and his friends a form of worship.

At Hilfield, an avenue of lime trees runs from the main buildings to the cemetery. Planted ten years before the first brothers arrived at the friary, they are now just coming into their prime. Tall and graceful, their trunks and branches frame the view and direct one's attention towards the valley below. They seem to me like the nave of a gothic cathedral that changes colour according to the natural seasons of the year: from the bare limbs of winter, through the soft greens of spring and the heavy viridian of high summer to a glorious golden autumn finale. Their leaves susurrate a chorus of praise. The medieval stonemasons incorporated this natural inbuilt praise in the foliage with which they decorated the pillars and window tracery of their churches.

Antoni Gaudí, the architect of the Sagrada Familia in Barcelona and a deeply religious person, followed the patterns inherent in the structures of nature; the pillars of the basilica lean off-perpendicular like the trees of a forest. The cathedral is an extraordinary construction that points the attention upwards, but it is of a very different conception from the Babel-like skyscrapers that today tower over cities around the world as statements of hubristic domination. To join Francis in the chorus of creation involves letting go our attempts to impose structures, systems and solutions on the world – architectural, economic, political, social or individual – and learning to sing in harmony with every creature.

In *Francis – A Life in Songs*, the poet Ann Wroe has given contemporary voice to the lyricism of Francis the troubadour in his relationship with all that is around him. Her poems are fine-tuned to an awareness that in encountering every creature, both animate and inanimate, there is the possibility of revelation – an unveiling of truth about oneself and about the world. It is a truth that poetry has served from time immemorial. There is a rabbinic midrash that emphasizes the crucial nature of poetry: '[God says] "Were it not for the poetry and song that they [all flesh and blood] recite before me daily, I would not have created the world"' (Fisch, 1988, p. 119). In the care of creation today, as well as needing scientists who understand the issues of climate change and biodiversity, and politicians, economists and sociologists who address human behaviour, we also need poets who speak truthfully and imaginatively. By doing so, they enable us to see differently and to join the song of the earth.

Union

For many without a religious affiliation, and for some with one, it's the romantic image of the young Francis portrayed in Zeffirelli's 1973 film, *Brother Sun, Sister Moon*, with its haunting music and lyrics by Donovan, that strikes a chord. Francis' singing amid fields of brilliant red poppies can evoke longing for a life connected with the natural world without the clutter of authorities and institutions, a return to Edenic innocence. But this portrayal is as untrue to the Francis presented in the first part of this book as it is unrealistic about life; or, rather, it plays Francis' song with all the harmonies left out. The message of Francis and the Franciscan tradition is not a call to worship nature (pantheism), which can become just as much an idol to us as the possession of consumer goods and the acquisition of power. For Francis, creation and everything in it points beyond itself to the outpouring and self-emptying Source of all (panentheism). It was through his pious intimacy with every creature, including wounded and broken human beings, that he was lured to the love of God.

It is significant that Francis composed his great Canticle of the Creatures towards the end of his life, at a time when he was in great pain from disease of the eyes and could hardly see the creatures whose song he was articulating. By then he had also surrendered leadership of the burgeoning order of friars, which to his sadness was already departing from his vision of minority and peace. It was in this darkness and loss that he found union with his Beloved. As many discover in the life of prayer, the journey into God is not about a steady growth of proficiency in techniques or an accumulation of spiritual experiences. In fact, it may well involve the feeling that we don't know how to pray at all. As Henry Vaughan writes, 'There is in God, some say, a deep but dazzling darkness' (Davie, 1981, p. 123). Contemplation is not so much gazing on God through our senses as it is living, silent and blinded, within God's loving and ever compassionate gaze.

Blessing

Francis blessed animals during his preaching and I have often been invited, or begged, to lead 'pet services' – presumably in the expectation that as a friar I should know what to do. I have to confess that it's not my favourite activity. I hold my hands over each animal that is brought to me, hoping that it's not going to be one about which I have a particular phobia. But it's not just animals that we are called to bless. In gratefully acknowledging and responding to God's blessing on the whole of creation, and in sharing that blessing with others, we return blessing to God. 'Blessing is the main thoroughfare for traffic between God and creatures, both human and non-human' (Davis, 2009, p. 27). Following Francis and the Franciscan tradition is about being caught up and carried along this thoroughfare.

In a chapel to the side of the Basilica of St Francis in Assisi is a small parchment that was given by Francis to his close companion Brother Leo in September 1224, shortly after Francis had received the stigmata, the wounds of Christ in his hands, feet and side. It's a precious document, not least because it's the only writing we have in Francis' own hand. On one side are written 'The Praises of God', which honour 39 attributes of God such as love, beauty, hope, joy, guardian. On the other is a blessing for Leo who at that time had been weighed down in despondency:

> May the Lord Bless you and keep you;
> May He show His face to you and be merciful to you.
> May He turn His countenance on you and give you peace.
>   (Num. 6.24–27)
> May the Lord bless you, Brother Leo. (I.112)

In the face of the serious crises of the world today the most profound response we can make is that of blessing. We bless as, with Francis, we pay loving attention to the economy of gift in which we live. We bless when we tread lightly and humbly on the planet, inhabiting it as our precious common home. We bless by acknowledging our interdependence with all things and by living justly and wisely in relation to each other. We bless as our lives bear witness to Francis' and Clare's alternative worldview, and when we join with them in thanksgiving and praise. In blessing we are blessed, and with all creation we return blessing to the Blessed One who is 'all good, supreme good, totally good' (I.162). Through blessing the face of the earth is renewed.

What the lives of the two friaries of Hilfield and Plaistow have to offer is not just a model of sustainability and conservation, nor simply a programme of social care. They are, rather, instances of places and their communities in which blessing is both a response to and an expression of an integral ecology – environmental, social, spiritual – 'held together' in God (Col. 1.17). The lives of both places, each in their own way, are songs of praise to God.

Questions for reflection

- What in the world do you weep over?
- Are there actions you are being called to undertake in response to the growing environmental crisis?
- What in your life at the present time resounds in tune with the song of creation?

Further reading

Naomi Klein, 2015, *This Changes Everything*, London: Penguin.

Frances Ward, 2020, *Like There's No Tomorrow: Climate Crisis, Eco-Anxiety and God*, Durham: Sacristy Press.

Ann Wroe, 2018, *Francis: A Life in Songs*, London: Jonathan Cape.

11

Relationship and Reconciliation

In January 2017 a meeting took place in London between representatives of world religions and two leading climate scientists from Imperial College London who were members of the United Nations Intergovernmental Panel on Climate Change. At that meeting, the scientists outlined evidence of warming in our planet's atmosphere, its human-related causes, and its possible future projection. They also gave estimates on this warming's likely effects on our natural environment and on human life's sustainability on earth. However, they noted that scientific evidence, though important, does not on its own persuade people to change behaviours and patterns of life. For the impending crisis to be averted, changes of heart and world-view are essential, they said: 'And that is why we are speaking with you as members of faith communities because you speak to hearts as well as to minds.'

This acknowledgement by senior scientists that our climate crisis is not simply a problem to be fixed by technology but is also a moral, theological and spiritual one is significant. Our book has been written in the belief that Francis of Assisi and the Franciscan tradition have an important contribution to make in transforming worldviews that have become dangerous to life and to all creation, both human and non-human.

'St Francis is the example par excellence of the care for the vulnerable and of an integral ecology lived out joyfully and authentically' (Francis, 2015, p. 11). In this concluding chapter, we tease out key points that the example of St Francis and his followers present to contemporary readers, demanding that we both see the world differently and act differently to reconcile humanity with creation.

Francis, creation and prayer

The soul is moved by heavenly love and longing when, having clearly beheld the beauty and the fairness of the Word of God, it falls deeply in love with His loveliness and receives from the Word Himself a certain dart and wound of love. For this Word is the image and splendour of the invisible God, the Firstborn of all creation, in whom were all things created that are in heaven and on earth, seen and unseen alike. If, then, a man can so extend his thinking as to ponder and consider the beauty and the grace of all the things that have been created in the Word, the very charm of them will so smite him, the grandeur of their brightness will so pierce him as with a chosen dart – as says the prophet (Is. 49.2) – that he will suffer from the dart Himself a saving wound, and will be kindled with the blessed fire of His love. (Origen, 1957, p. 29)

It has often been suggested that poverty, humility and simplicity are the foundations of Francis of Assisi's life, both spiritual and physical. While there is clearly truth in this, these foundations are surely themselves underpinned by the solid rock of prayer. As a very young man, at the start of his journey from apprentice businessman to friar and later saint, he spent much time in caves and woods around Assisi, often accompanied by a single companion whose name we do not know (I.187). From this time of prayer and inner exploration came the inspiration that led to the next step in his journey of transformation: action at San Damiano through repairing the ruined church (II.536).

As we noted earlier, by the end of his life Francis was spending up to half his time in prayer, particularly silent contemplative prayer inhabiting remote hermitages. We have also seen numerous examples of creation inspiring Francis to pray and draw close to God. These include the cricket that sang praises with Francis, the little water-bird at Rieti that sat in his lap while he prayed, and the Canticle of Creation, perhaps the culmination of all his prayers. The evidence suggests that creation became part of prayer for Francis and drew him to

Christ, that he saw the Word present in every creature and came to have 'knowledge of the speech' of creation (*The Way of a Pilgrim*, 1965, p. 42).

Such knowledge and seeing of creation has been evident in our exploration of the Franciscans who came after Francis and developed his lived creation spirituality. We have seen how contemplative attention, even in a developed urban environment, can lead to a deeper recognition of God's presence in the world. As described by Duns Scotus, truly to know and delight in the this-ness, uniqueness and value of each component of creation is surely the fruit of prayer in contemplation of God's love within all creation.

Living in prayer with devotion, thanksgiving and praise to God, compassion for suffering, and reconciliation with all returned Francis to a 'state of innocence' and friendship with God. Ultimately this led to his physical transformation in receiving the wounds of Christ in his body as stigmata, all in the context of a deeply prayerful experience of union with God. Understanding this, it becomes easier to see how Francis, in the long tradition of Christian holy people, might calm wild wolves or inspire whole flocks of birds to listen silently to his preaching. As long ago as the seventh century, Isaac of Nineveh experienced this:

> The humble man approaches ravening beasts, and when their gaze rests upon him, their wildness is tamed. They come up to him as to their Master, wag their heads and tails, and lick his hands and feet, for they smell coming from him that same scent that exhaled from Adam before the Fall, when they were gathered together before him and he gave them names in Paradise. (Isaac the Syrian, 2011, p. 536)

The spiritual journey in prayer is intended ultimately to lead to union with God (Nichols, 2019) which in turn leads to seeing creation differently. 'As for the saints, it is in God that they receive awareness of created objects. They see the world in God, permeated by his light and forming a whole in the hollow of his hand' (Clément, 1993, p. 225). Such a world, pregnant with God, as Angela of Foligno memorably put it, has nothing profane in it. All is sacred, from the most everyday items and the smallest creatures to the tallest trees and highest mountains. Simple scraps of paper with words on became holy for Francis, to be treated with respect as they might carry God's Word, both spiritually and physically. He wrote: 'Wherever the names and written words of the Lord may be found in unclean places, let them be gathered up and placed in a becoming place' (I.54).

Although the classic description of prayer ends in union, the pathway is notoriously hard from initial purgation through illumination. We have seen, particularly in the writings of Jacopone da Todi and Angela of Foligno, how tough, dark and lengthy that journey can be, through suffering and grief. But we have also seen descriptions of wonderful times of illumination, seeing glimpses of God: light, loving, sweet. In deep prayer, the soul 'drowns' in the immensity of God and truly participates in creation, experiencing all life as a loving unity.

We can follow Francis of Assisi's example by rooting ourselves in prayer and so be drawn close in relationship to God and into the sacredness of all that is. Knowing this in our lives will, in turn, demand that we see differently and, if we are to follow Francis fully, act differently to reconcile humanity with creation. It is not an easy route, but there is a long history of people taking this path. That they continue to do so is evident in the witness of contemporary Franciscans throughout our world. By choosing this route, we actively participate in the work of the Spirit, reconciling the world to God, renewing the whole of creation.

Francis, creation and action

The occasion when Francis felt torn between living in contemplative hermitage prayer and a life of worldly activity as an evangelist, noted earlier, is a significant example in the Franciscan story (II.622–4). It contains several features still evident in Franciscan spirituality today, particularly relating to creation.

First, despite being an experienced leader and holy man, Francis asked for advice from two others: Sister Clare and Brother Sylvester. Today we might call them his spiritual companions or directors. Listening to others and taking their advice, both those we look up to and those less experienced than ourselves, is central to the spiritual life. It forms the basis of all relationship and hence of all reconciliation. St Benedict famously began his Rule with 'Listen ... and take ... to heart' (Benedict, 2008, p. 1). Francis began his *Earlier Rule* of 1221 with the words: 'The rule and life of these brothers is this, namely: "to live in obedience, in chastity, and without anything of their own," and to follow the teaching and footprints of our Lord Jesus Christ' (I.63). Obedience was the first step in following Jesus, the willingness to disinvest in oneself and become a lesser brother to all. As we have seen, relationship and reconciliation are key segments of any Franciscan spirituality of creation. They call us to listen to others and to the needs of all God's creation, to see differently, and then to change or act if needed.

Francis took the advice he received as a command and immediately set off to preach. Such immediacy was a mark of his radical commitment to following in the way of Jesus Christ: none of the mulling it over and making long lists of pros and cons that we might indulge in, simply 'let's do it'. Francis was a man both of action and of prayer. The action in this case was the Franciscan priority of preaching, following the risen Christ's injunction: 'Go into the world and proclaim the good news to the whole creation' (Mark 16.15). Francis used to say that this priority of preaching 'must move people's hearts and lift them up to spiritual joy' (II.186). It had to be undertaken humbly but not necessarily through words. 'Let all the brothers preach by their deeds' (I.75), he instructed, and 'let the brothers preach in every way' (I.89), including singing and praising.

When directed by his advisers to preach, Francis girded himself and took to the roads, running swiftly. Where we today might take a suitcase of clothes and so on, we have seen that 'girding himself' for Francis meant simply one habit and pair of sandals for the journey. No baggage enabled light and swift travelling. Committed to poverty, simplicity, dispossession and the powerlessness of minority, he lived this action to the extreme and encouraged his followers to do the same.

That the good news is to be proclaimed to 'the whole creation' is also significant in Franciscan spirituality. We have heard much of delight, joy, thankfulness, praise and singing but we have also explored the Fall, including humankind's taking dominion over all creation and turning away to sin: pride leading to greed leading to disobedience, as Bonaventure wrote. The Franciscan story includes experiencing tears, darkness and lament, both spiritually and physically. Francis wept for his sins and his failure to respond to love. Angela of Foligno told of anger, despair and fear of abandonment, and searching, as Francis did, for Christ among poor and suffering people, particularly people with leprosy. Jacopone da Todi sang from the depths of his grief and suffering, lamenting the loss of the sense of God's presence.

Having taken to the roads to preach, Francis received 'new strength from heaven'. In the Christian story, resurrection and redemption always follow fall. However desperate things look, there is always that hope: for Franciscans, penance and turnaround follow tears and lament. We have noted throughout this book that God, Father, Son and Spirit, are experienced in the Franciscan tradition through Scripture and prayer and throughout creation. Once he had committed himself to give up all things, Christ was everywhere for Francis, particularly in the Eucharist – the celebration of Christ's acceptance of suffering and death as the way to new life.

Stories such as this one are so significant in Franciscan experience because Francis did not leave us a well thought through text, theology or spirituality to guide us. He simply left the model of his life, a lived spirituality as recorded by historians, along with a few writings, mostly instructions or Rules for his fraternity and prayers composed of extracts from Scripture. Key features of Francis' lived example in relation to creation include: prayer; caring for others; dispossession; powerlessness; respectful, peaceful and reciprocal relationships; reconciliation;

being alongside, connected with and preaching to all creation; discovering God at every Eucharist while seeing all of creation as sacramental; reverence for precious places; praise, joy, thanksgiving and blessing; tears, penance and forgiveness.

We have explored how some of Francis' followers, from medieval Umbria to twenty-first-century England, have developed his example and allowed it to shape their thinking and living. The 'lived spirituality' of Francis and those who have followed can guide our contemporary vision and allow us to see differently. It has inspired modern prophetic figures to call for change and action through the integration of human relationships: interpersonal, environmental and divine.

Living Franciscan action today: an integrated ecology

For followers of Francis, relationship is everything. Living a spirituality of creation centres on living in 'right relationship' with all creation: respect, reciprocity and reconciliation built on love, delight and minority, leaving behind power and possessiveness. Underpinning that relationship with creation is our relationship with our divine Creator, itself rooted in prayer. Drawing close to our loving Father in prayer is the rock on which all Franciscan experience and spirituality are built. We have seen something of how hard this can be in lament, tears and purgation but we have also touched on joy in praise, blessing, harmony, illumination and union.

Prayer is always linked to action for Franciscans. Throughout this book we have explored the practicalities of living this out, from Francis' example of caring for other people and for non-human creation along with preaching, through to the actions and lived experience of his contemporary followers. We have shared something of the journey made by the Franciscans at Hilfield Friary from a place of prayer, welcome, hospitality, retreat and care for vulnerable people to a community that, in addition to these important activities, lives an integrated ecology in relationship with and reconciled to its environment.

The phrase 'integrated ecology', originating from pioneering

Franciscan work in a Brazilian slum community (Boff, 1997), links environmental, social and spiritual factors. It informed Pope Francis' prophetic call to all humanity for an end to the unsustainable modern myth of unlimited material progress in a finite world, and for dialogue and cooperation 'as instruments of God for the care of creation' (Francis, 2015, p. 13).

Such integration brings environmental, social and spiritual factors into our own relationships. How we relate to the land and where we live, how we relate to each other and how we relate to God are one and the same, of equal and fundamental importance to our existence as part of creation. Any break in this connectedness between human beings and earth requires reconciliation (Boff, 1997, p. 81). Additionally, the reflection of God's love seen in the this-ness of a cricket or a grain of sand needs integrating and reconciling with a wider ecology, economically, environmentally, socially, culturally and within daily life. All are significant for our continued presence on this planet and to a vision of how true wholeness of life in Jesus Christ might be.

Drawing this book to a close, the challenge for each of us, and for all humanity, is first to hear the instruction given to St Francis to 'repair my house' as it applies to each of us. This involves accepting that the house in need of repair is the whole of God's creation on this planet, and that we have an ethical obligation to correct the ecological injustices in creation that humanity has caused (Boff, 1997, p. 132). If the Covid-19 pandemic of 2020 with all its many consequences has taught us anything, it must be that we cannot self-isolate from God's creation (Carney, 2020). We are an integral and interconnected part of this world with corresponding responsibilities for its care, past, present and future.

Second, we need to demonstrate repairing this damaged creation in our own lives. Such practical ecological theology must involve those twin Franciscan demands of prayer and action, integrating the 'being' of our own spirituality and relationship with our maker alongside the 'doing' of peacefully and reciprocally reconciling our existence within all creation, animate and inanimate, human and animal, rich and poor.

From such reconciled and right and loving relationships flow the Franciscan imperatives of justice and peace, as Duns Scotus pointed out so long ago, echoed more recently by Pope Francis.

Each person's journey is unique and each begins with a single step. The lived experiences of Franciscans and others at Hilfield and elsewhere outlined throughout this book contain many examples of possible first steps. Taking steps like this, following in the way of Francis of Assisi, is being prophetic. Franciscan prophecy has been described as 'soft prophecy' (Rohr, 2014, p. 41) – defined as the prophecy of a way of life that is counter to the ways of the world. Few of us can offer the 'hard prophecy' of Pope Francis, Leonardo Boff or Greta Thunberg.

It is beyond the scope of our volume to explore more fully those many potential steps that might be undertaken in response to this challenge in varying contexts. These might, for example, be within everyday life, through work to sustain our environment, or engaging in awareness raising, protest or international negotiation. There is a large literature available in which you can explore possibilities for your life: see our suggestions for further reading below.

As we write, lockdowns and travel restrictions across the nations in response to the worldwide pandemic caused by the coronavirus have given our planet a breather from the damaging effects of humanity. The earth, so often described as fragile, is also robust: after only a few weeks it was already bouncing back with bird and fish numbers rising, pollution levels falling by staggering amounts, air clearing and blue sky becoming visible above cities. We pray that this sudden unexpected shock to us all, allied with the example of Francis of Assisi and his followers over the centuries, will make all people and nations see their relationship to the world differently and then act to reconcile humanity with God's great gift of all creation.

Postscript

The ancient city of Spoleto, south of Assisi, is surrounded by the Apennine mountains, on whose slopes lies the holy forest of Monteluco (from *lucus* meaning sacred woods). Following fourth-century Syrian and later Benedictine monks, Francis of Assisi established a hermitage here in 1218 alongside an ancient chapel dedicated to St Catherine of Alexandria. The early brothers' very plain and simple cells can still be seen, surrounded by today's Sanctuary. Significant Franciscan figures have lived here including St Bernardine of Siena, an inspirational fifteenth-century leader, and St Anthony of Padua, a contemporary of Francis who stayed in a nearby cave. This friary in the woods remains a precious place for Franciscans.

At the start of his spiritual journey, Francis focused on repairing just one 'precious place': San Damiano near Assisi. He went on to repair others but never wished to possess them, simply to live, pray and work in them. The records tell us that in the latter part of his life he spent up to half the year in retreat and prayer in various hermitages. These precious places inspired him (I.125), as they have inspired many Christians since, and he came to see all God's creation, animate and inanimate, as precious.

Our hope, as we end this book, is that you, the reader, have been led to review, reflect and pray about the precious place that is the planet we are privileged to have been given to occupy at present. The example of Francis of Assisi's relationship with all God's gift of creation, along with that of his followers today and over the centuries, has inspired each of us. In particular, we have each been led to review our care for, reconciliation with, and repair of that part of creation of which we have been given temporary stewardship. We pray that our words encourage you also to see differently and in turn to be inspired to live, pray and act differently.

May the Lord give you peace.

Questions for reflection

- What actions might you undertake in response to the challenge of our moral obligation to repair God's creation?
- How could you re-vision and change your life to participate in the ecological conversion demanded by Pope Francis?
- Which places are precious to you and how might you use them differently?

Further reading

Leonardo Boff, 1997, *Cry of the Earth, Cry of the Poor*, trans. Philip Berryman, New York: Orbis Books.

The Cry of the Earth and the Cries of the Poor: An OFM Study Guide on the Care of Creation, available free from https://ofm.org//wp-content/uploads/2016/07/CuraCreato-EN.pdf.

Ilia Delio, Keith Warner and Pamela Wood, 2008, *Care for Creation: A Franciscan Spirituality of the Earth*, Cincinnati, OH: St Anthony Messenger Press.

Pope Francis, 2015, *Laudato Si': On Care for Our Common Home*, available free from www.vatican.va/content/francesco/en/encyclicals/documents/papa-francesco_20150524_enciclica-laudato-si.html.

Joanna Macy and Chris Johnstone, 2012, *Active Hope: How to Face the Mess We're in Without Going Crazy*, Novato, CA: New World Library.

Dawn Nothwehr OSF, 2012, *Ecological Footprints: An Essential Franciscan Guide for Faith and Sustainable Living*, Collegeville, MN: Liturgical Press.

Susan Sayers, 2019, *This? How Christians Respond to Climate Change*, Stowmarket: Kevin Mayhew.

Stephen Snow, 2019, *The Green Light*, Edale: Whitmore.

Nicholas Spencer and Robert White, 2007, *Christianity, Climate Change and Sustainable Living*, London: SPCK.

Appendix

Studying Francis

In studying Francis and his followers, we have to acknowledge our distance from what actually happened during their lifetimes. Sources often cannot be taken as literal records of exactly what Francis said or did in a particular situation. Sometimes there are several versions of the same story, making study complex but allowing historical analysis.

An example is Francis' interaction for eight days with an obedient singing cricket, explored in Chapter 2. The version quoted (II.357) was written in about 1246 by friar Thomas of Celano, Francis' first official biographer. It is from *The Remembrance of the Desire of a Soul*, also known as *The Second Life of Saint Francis*. Unlike his *First Life of Saint Francis*, dated 1229, which aimed to be a detailed biography, Thomas' later concern was to add newly available material and develop ideals. Through this, he hoped to help, in their everyday living, the many brothers now in the fraternity who had never met Francis (II.234–6).

The singing cricket appears again in the *Assisi Compilation* (II.218). This group of stories, which overlaps with another work known as *The Legend of Perugia*, was collected over several years, most likely between 1244 and 1260. Its authorship is uncertain but it may be the memories of some of Francis' earliest companions, Brothers Leo, Angelo and Rufino, who often begin their anecdotes with the words 'we who were with him'.

The cricket reappears in *The Major Legend of Saint Francis*, dated 1260–63 (II.593), a comprehensive record of Francis' life by St Bonaventure. Aiming to unify factions within the brotherhood, he went on to order the destruction of all previous biographies in a largely successful attempt to make his the only authorized and authoritative work. Fortunately, some original manuscripts survived this episode, many discovered since the end of the nineteenth century. This means that for today's student of Francis and Franciscanism navigating the various sources can be very confusing.

Study is also influenced by the many historical differences between Francis' world and ours. For example, the life of Francis and his contemporaries was shaped by a religious worldview: steeped in Scripture narrative, informed by Christian tradition, and to a large extent controlled by Church hierarchy. Even though changes were afoot in challenging Church authority and a more secular culture was emerging, the veil between sacred and secular in Francis' time was very thin. A scientific approach to the natural world, such as isolating and objectifying animate and inanimate creatures in order to understand and use them – seventeenth-century Europe's foundation for developing enlightenment thought – was unknown to him.

Another complication for contemporary readers is medieval writers' frequent use of embellishment, which was quite usual at the time. Many stories evolved as oral and written history was told and retold after Francis died. In the years immediately following his death, there were political reasons to portray Francis as virtuous and heading for perfection. Accurately recording one man's life became less important than portraying his story as a saint to fit with papal objectives of reform and renewal throughout the whole Church.

Retelling and embellishing incidents concerning holy people and others is known as hagiography, which often involves representing people as much better than they really are, putting them on a pedestal, idealizing them or treating them with undue reverence. There is no doubt that this happened in writings about Francis in the century after his death, and continues to happen. In this book, our aim has been to examine many of the stories about Francis and creation so that underlying meanings have emerged from the breadth of material included, despite the inevitable embellishments.

Further reading

William R. Hugo, 2011, *Studying the Life of Saint Francis of Assisi: A Beginner's Workbook*, New York: New City Press.

Glossary

Acts of the Process of Canonization

'The official Church record of all evidence and testimony of witnesses in the process of deciding if a person should be listed among the canonized saints of the Church' (Nothwehr, 2002, p. 453).

Chapter

'The council or meeting of Religious to deliberate and make decisions about the community is known as a Chapter. In some orders, this may consist of all the professed members of the community; in others, the Chapter is a group of members elected by the community as a whole to be their representatives' (Kirkpatrick et al., 2009, p. 212).

Contemplation

'Religiously contemplation sometimes refers to meditation. But the chief concern here is with contemplation as an intensification of a transforming awareness of divine presence. Contemplation transforms one's spiritual resources and effects a deeper practice of virtue' (Sheldrake, 2005, p. 211).

Contuition

'In its specific sense, contuition implies an indirect knowledge of God in his effects. It is an intuitive type of knowledge of God whereby God is perceived in the created world without the aid of exterior senses. It is a sense of the presence of God together with the consciousness of created being, an awareness of the ontological presence of God attained in the consciousness of being. In the context of exemplary causality, it implies the awareness of simultaneity of form in the created thing and in the original or eternal exemplar' (Delio, 2001, p. 199).

Devotion

'The orientation of the soul to God through the spiritual gifts of humility and piety. It is a habit of the soul by which grace enables the soul to be turned to God and to Christ through the raising up of one's mind and heart to God' (Delio, 2001, p. 200).

Emanation

'Emanation describes the activity of God as the *summum*, or First Principle, characterized by what Bonaventure calls "fountain-fulness" (*fontalis plenitudo*) ... The Franciscan's insistence on the fecundity of the Father as the source of all production – first, the emanation of the Word and the Spirit in the Trinity, and then the creation of the universe – is the foundation of his theological metaphysics' (McGinn, 1998, p. 88).

Exemplarisim and Exemplar

'Exemplarism is the doctrine of relations of expression between God and creatures. God is the exemplary cause of all things, because God in knowing himself expresses his most perfect idea, the *rationes* or the eternal patterns of all possible things. Everything that exists, therefore, is in some way related to God as a copy or imitation. Bonaventure distinguishes three different degrees of resemblance: the vestige, image and similitude. The exemplar is the pattern or original model in whose likeness all things are made. It is the basis of imitation. Because the Word expresses the Father's ideas, the Word is the exemplar of all that exists' (Delio, 2001, p. 200).

Friars Minor

'From the Italian word for "brother", the word "friar" became universally used for all those who joined the Order founded by Francis. But Francis gave his followers the particular designation of "the Lesser Brothers", or "Minores", to indicate that they should see themselves as having no rights or privileges, but only living a life of penury and extreme simplicity. It was also a noteworthy play on words when paralleled with the terminology used in the small city of Assisi, where those privileged to reside within the city walls were called the Majores, or Greater Ones, whilst those living outside the walls were termed the Minores, or Lesser Ones. Francis seems clearly to have aligned his community with the "excluded" rather than the "included"' (Kirkpatrick, 2009, p. 216).

Friary

'The designation of a place where the Friars lived and from which they went out. In the beginning, these were termed Convents, but as the followers of Francis began simply to be known as friars, or more particularly Franciscan friars, their places of residence became redesignated as Friaries' (Kirkpatrick, 2009, p. 216).

Haecceitas

'From [the Latin] *haec* (literally *this*); the individuating principle of each being; the ultimate reality of the being' (Ingham, 2003, p. 228).

Individuation, principle of

'That which makes a thing what it is and not another' (Ingham, 2003, p. 229).

Mendicant spirituality

'Innovative religious movements of the thirteenth century embraced a form of life that emphasized poverty and included begging alms (*mendicare* in Latin), giving them the name of "mendicant" communities. Their members were known as "friars" (brothers), often identified by the colour of their habit. By 1210 these included the Friars Minor or Franciscans (Grey Friars) and the Friars Preacher or Dominicans (Black Friars)' (Sheldrake, 2005, p. 435).

Metaphysics

'Philosophers traditionally regarded as metaphysicians have in common that they attempt to provide and to justify an account of the most basic constituents of reality, and the manner in which these are related to one another ... such as matter, mind, space, time and cause; and of whether the existence, nature and interrelation of such entities provide reasons for thinking that God does or does not exist, or clues as to his nature' (Richardson, 1983, p. 361).

Midrash

An ancient form of textual interpretation of the Hebrew Scriptures, commenting on the words and letters of the text, and exploring the unwritten spaces in the recorded narratives. A way of questioning the text and looking for new layers of meaning.

Minister

'Ministers have the care and charge of brothers and sisters in a Province (Minister Provincial) or of the whole Order (Minister General). Francis deliberately chose the terms Minister and Guardian in direct contrast to Superior, Abbot and Prior, indicating that those in positions of leadership in the Order should be seen as servants of the community' (Kirkpatrick, 2009, p. 217).

Mysticism/mystics

'Those elements in Christian belief and practice that concern the preparation for, the consciousness of, and the effects attendant upon a heightened awareness of God's immediate and transforming presence. Since God cannot be present the way a created thing in the universe is present, many mystics insist that true consciousness of God is best realized through absence, that is, through a process of negation that strips away all experiences, images and concepts to aim toward the mystery that lies beyond both affirmation and negation' (Sheldrake, 2005, p. 19).

Office/Daily Office/Divine Office

'The round of liturgical services of prayer and worship, which mark the rhythm of the daily routine in the Religious Life, is called the Office. Religious communities may use the services laid down by the Church or may have their own particular office book. The offices may be called Morning, Midday, Evening and Night Prayer, or may be referred to by their more traditional names, such as Matins, Lauds, Terce, Sext, None, Vespers and Compline. There might also be a separate Office of Readings' (Kirkpatrick, 2009, p. 218).

Participation

'Refers to the way creatures can share in or possess the life of God. It is a mode of possession in which what is possessed is received from another who is essentially different. In a proper sense, participation refers only to human beings since only they can consciously share in the life of God through grace' (Delio, 2001, p. 202).

Penance

'The word derives from the Latin *paenitentia*, meaning penitence or repentance. In Christian history it has variously designated an inner turning to God or a public returning to the church, any of a series of ecclesiastical disciplines designed to facilitate such inward or outward reconversion, and the various works that had to be performed as part of such disciplines' (Richardson, 1983, p. 435).

Religious

'The general term for a person living the Religious Life, whether monk, nun, friar, brother, sister etc.' (Kirkpatrick, 2009, p. 220).

Self-diffusive

'From "diffuse" which is to pour out and to permit or cause something to spread out. Goodness is not self contained, but rather by its very nature, causes itself to move outward towards others' (Nothwehr, 2002, p. 463).

Society of St Francis

An Anglican religious community drawn together in 1937 from various Franciscan communities, made up of a First Order of brothers (SSF) and sisters (CSF), a Second Order of contemplative sisters inspired by St Clare (OSC), and a Third Order of men and women living in the spirit of St Francis but not in community (TSSF). See websites listed in the bibliography.

Spiritual Senses

'Inner senses of the spirit – touch, taste, sight, smell and hearing – by which the soul can perceive the presence of God. As spiritual gifts, they are the fruit of wisdom attained in union with Christ, and are integral to the contemplation of God. As eternal Word, God is seen and the harmony of the Word is heard; as incarnate Word, God's wisdom is tasted and his love is embraced; as inspired Word, God's fragrance is inhaled' (Delio, 2001, p. 202).

Stigmata

The crucifixion wounds of Jesus in his hands, feet and side, said to have been formed also in the body of Francis of Assisi during a retreat at La Verna in 1224.

Wisdom

'Experiential knowledge of God deepened by love whereby charity renders the soul a divine similitude through the unitive power proper to love. As the fullness of love, it is an interior "tasting", or delighting in the divine. It delights in God as good in the interior of the soul and sees the right ordering of all things in the book of creation. As the uncreated and incarnate Word, Christ is the book of wisdom. Supreme wisdom is revealed in the cross of Jesus Christ' (Delio, 2001, p. 202).

Bibliography

All quotations from the works of Francis and the early documents are taken from *Francis of Assisi: Early Documents*, edited by Regis J. Armstrong, J. A. Wayne Hellmann and William J. Short (1999–2001, New York: New City Press): Volume I *The Saint*; Volume II *The Founder*; Volume III *The Prophet*. Used by permission. Quotations from these volumes are given as volume number and page number in the text (e.g. I.1 is Volume I, page 1). All three are available free online through the Commission on the Franciscan Intellectual Tradition at www.francis cantradition.org.

Anderson, Inger, 2020, 'Coronaviruses: are they here to stay?', *UN Environment Programme*, www.unenvironment.org/news-and-stories/story/coronaviruses-are-they-here-stay (accessed 25.6.20).

Angela of Foligno, 1993, *The Book of the Blessed Angela of Foligno* in *Angela of Foligno: Complete Works*, Classics of Western Spirituality, trans. Paul Lachance OFM, New York: Paulist Press.

Armstrong, Edward A., 1973, *Saint Francis: Nature Mystic – The Derivation and Significance of the Nature Stories in the Franciscan Legend*, Berkeley, CA: University of California Press.

Armstrong, Regius J., 2006, *Clare of Assisi: Early Documents, The Lady*, New York: New City Press.

A Rocha UK, www.arocha.org.uk (accessed 7.5.20).

Augustine of Hippo, 2004, *Saint Augustine: Exposition of the Psalms*, vol. 6, trans. Maria Boulding OSB, Boniface Ramsey (ed.), New York: New City Press.

Balthasar, Hans Urs von, 1961, *Prayer*, trans. A. V. Littledale, London: SPCK.

Barrett Browning, Elizabeth, *Aurora Leigh VII*, at http://digital.library.upenn.edu/women/barrett/aurora/aurora-7.html (accessed 7.5.20).

Bate, Jonathan, 2000, *The Song of the Earth*, London: Picador.

Bauckham, Richard, 2010, *Bible and Ecology: Rediscovering the Community of Creation*, London: Darton, Longman and Todd.

Benedict, 2008, *The Rule of Benedict*, trans. C. White, London: Penguin.

Berry, Wendell, 2012, '2012 Jefferson Lecture with Wendell

Berry', *National Endowment for the Humanities*, www.neh.gov/ news/2012-jefferson-lecture-wendell-berry (accessed 7.5.20).

Boff, Leonardo, 1997, *Cry of the Earth, Cry of the Poor*, trans. Philip Berryman, New York: Orbis Books.

Bonaventure, 1960, *The Triple Way (De Triplici Via), or Love Enkindled (Incendium Amoris)*, from *The Works of Bonaventure*, Vol. 1, *Mystical Opuscula*, trans. José de Vinck, Paterson, NJ: St Anthony Guild Press.

————, 1963, *The Works of Bonaventure*, Vol. 2, *The Breviloquium*, trans. José de Vinck, Paterson, NJ: St Anthony Guild Press.

————, 1970, *Collations on the Six Days, The Works of Bonaventure*, Vol. 5, trans. José de Vinck, Paterson, NJ: St Anthony Guild Press.

————, 1978, *Bonaventure: The Soul's Journey into God; The Tree of Life; The Life of St. Francis*, Classics of Western Spirituality, trans. Ewert Cousins, London: SPCK.

Bookless, Dave, 2010, *God Doesn't do Waste*, Nottingham: IVP.

Carney, Mark, 2020, 'By Invitation', *The Economist*, 16 April, www.economist.com/by-invitation/ (accessed 7.5.20).

The Catechism of the Catholic Church, www.vatican.va>archive> ENG0015 (accessed 7.5.20).

Christian Aid, 2017, *An Unquenchable Thirst for More – Faith and Economic Growth*, www.christianaid.org.uk (accessed 7.5.20).

Christie, Douglas E., 2012, *The Blue Sapphire of the Mind: Notes for a Contemplative Ecology*, Oxford: Oxford University Press.

Chryssavgis, John, 2019, *Creation as Sacrament: Reflections on Ecology and Spirituality*, London: T & T Clark.

Clément, Olivier, 1993, *The Roots of Christian Mysticism*, London: New City.

Common Worship: Services and Prayers for the Church of England, 2000, London: Church House Publishing.

Common Worship: Times and Seasons, 2006, London: Church House Publishing.

The Cry of the Earth and the Cries of the Poor: an OFM study guide on the care of creation, Rome 2016, available at https://ofm.org//wp-content/uploads/2016/07/CuraCreato-EN.pdf (accessed 28.4.20).

The Daily Office SSF, 2010, London: Mowbray.

Dalarun, Jacques, 2016, *The Canticle of Brother Sun: Francis of Assisi Reconciled*, trans. Philippe Yates, St Bonaventure University, NY: Franciscan Institute Publications.

Dante, Alighieri, 2006, *The Divine Comedy*, trans. Robin Kirkpatrick, London: Penguin.

Davie, Donald, 1981, *The New Oxford Book of Christian Verse*, Oxford: Oxford University Press.

Davis, Ellen F., 2009, *Scripture, Culture and Agriculture – An Agrarian Reading of Scripture*, Cambridge: Cambridge University Press.

_____, 2019, *Opening Israel's Scriptures*, Oxford: Oxford University Press.

Delio, Ilia, OSF, 2001, *Simply Bonaventure: An Introduction to His Life, Thought, and Writings*, New York: New City Press.

_____, 2003, *A Franciscan View of Creation: Learning to Live in a Sacramental World*, New York: The Franciscan Institute.

Delio, Ilia, OSF, Keith Douglass Warner OFM and Pamela Wood, 2008, *Care for Creation: A Franciscan Spirituality of the Earth*, Cincinnati, OH: St Anthony Messenger Press.

Doyle, Eric, OFM, 1997, *St Francis and the Song of Brotherhood and Sisterhood*, St Bonaventure University, NY: Franciscan Institute Publications.

Draper, Brian, 2012, *Less is More: Spirituality for Busy Lives*, Oxford: Lion Hudson.

Dunstan, Petà, 1997, *This Poor Sort: A History of the European Province of the Society of St Francis*, London: Darton, Longman and Todd.

Evagrius Ponticus, 1972, *The Praktikos and Chapters on Prayer*, Kalamazoo, MI: Cistercian Publications.

Fisch, Harold, 1988, *Poetry with a Purpose: Biblical Poetics and Interpretation*, Indianapolis, IN: Indiana University Press.

Frances Teresa OSC, 1995, *This Living Mirror: Reflections on Clare of Assisi*, London: Darton, Longman and Todd.

Francis, Pope, 2015, *Laudato si': On Care for Our Common Home*, www.vatican.va/content/francesco/en/encyclicals/documents/papa-francesco_20150524_enciclica-laudato-si.html (accessed 8.5.20).

Gilbert, Bob, 2018, *Ghost Trees: Nature and People in a London Parish*, London: Saraband.

Hammond, Jay M. (ed.), 2004, *Francis of Assisi – History, Hagiography and Hermeneutics in the Early Documents*, New York: New City Press.

Hayes, Zachary, OFM, 1997, *A Window to the Divine: Creation Theology*, Winona, MN: Anselm Academic.

Helen Julian CSF, 2020, *Franciscan Footprints: Following Christ in the ways of Francis and Clare*, Abingdon: Bible Reading Fellowship.

Hilfield Friary, www.hilfieldfriary.org.uk.

Hopkins, Gerard Manley, 1970, *The Poems of Gerard Manley Hopkins*, W. H. Gardner and N. H. MacKenzie (eds), Oxford: Oxford University Press.

Horan, Daniel P., OFM, 2018, *All God's Creatures: A Theology of Creation*, Lanham, MD: Lexington Books/Fortress Academic.

House, Adrian, 2000, *Francis of Assisi*, London: Pimlico.

Hugo, William R., 2011, *Studying the Life of Saint Francis of Assisi: A Beginner's Workbook*, 2nd edn, New York: New City Press.

Ingham, Mary Beth, 2003, *Scotus for Dunces: An Introduction to the Subtle Doctor*, St Bonaventure, New York: Franciscan Institute Publications.

Isaac the Syrian, 2011, Homily 77 in *Ascetical Homilies of Saint Isaac the Syrian*, trans. Holy Transfiguration Monastery, 2nd edn, Boston, MA.

Jacopone da Todi, 1982, *Jacopone da Todi: The Lauds*, trans. Serge and Elizabeth Hughes, Classics of Western Spirituality, New York: Paulist Press.

Julian of Norwich, 1998, *Revelations of Divine Love*, trans. Elizabeth Spearing, London: Penguin.

Jung, Carl Justav, 1956, *Symbols of Transformation, Collected Works 5*, New York: Pantheon.

Kirkpatrick, Damian, SSF, Philip Doherty OFM Conv., Sheelagh O'Flynn FMDM, 2009, *Joy in All Things: A Franciscan Companion*, new international edn, Norwich: Canterbury Press.

Klein, Naomi, 2015, *This Changes Everything*, London: Penguin.

Leclerc, Eloi, OFM, 1977, *The Canticle of Creatures: Symbols of Union*, trans. Matthew J. O'Connell, Chicago, IL: Franciscan Herald Press.

Louth, Andrew, 1981, *The Origins of the Christian Mystical Tradition: From Plato to Denys*, Oxford: Clarendon Press.

Macy, Joanna and Chris Johnstone, 2012, *Active Hope: How to Face the Mess We're in Without Going Crazy*, Novato, CA: New World Library.

McCarthy, Michael, 2010, *Say Goodbye to the Cuckoo: Migratory Birds and the Impending Ecological Catastrophe*, London: John Murray.

McGinn, Bernard, 1998, *The Flowering of Mysticism: Men and Women in the New Mysticism – 1200–1350*, The Presence of God: A History of Western Christian Mysticism Vol. 3, New York: Crossroad.

Migrateful, www.migrateful.org (accessed 7.5.20).

Moloney, Brian, 2013, *Francis of Assisi and His Canticle of Brother Sun Reassessed*, New York: Palgrave Macmillan.

National Biodiversity Network, *The State of Nature 2019*, www.nbn. org.uk (accessed 7.5.20).

Nichol, John, 2018, *Spitfire*, London: Simon and Schuster.

Nichols, Aidan, 2019, *The Word Invites: A Spiritual Theology*, Leominster: Gracewing.

Nothwehr, Dawn M., OSF (ed.), 2002, *Franciscan Theology of the Environment: An Introductory Reader*, Quincy, IL: Franciscan Press.

———, 2012, *Ecological Footprints: An Essential Franciscan Guide for Faith and Sustainable Living*, Collegeville, MN: Liturgical Press.

Origen, 1957, *The Song of Songs Commentary and Homilies*, trans. R. P. Lawson, Ancient Christian Writers, London: Longmans, Green and Co.

Osborne, Kenan B., OFM (ed.), 1994, *The History of Franciscan Theology*, St Bonaventure, New York: The Franciscan Institute.

Osuna, Francisco de, 1981, *The Third Spiritual Alphabet*, trans. Mary E. Giles, Classics of Western Spirituality, New York: Paulist Press.

Peck, George T., 1980, *The Fool of God: Jacopone da Todi*, Tuscaloosa, AL: University of Alabama Press.

Pitchford, Susan, 2006, *Following Francis: The Franciscan Way for Everyone*, Harrisburg, PA: Morehouse Publishing.

Porete, Marguerite, 1993, *The Mirror of Simple Souls*, trans. Ellen L. Babinsky, Classics of Western Spirituality, New York: Paulist Press.

Ramon, Brother, 1994, *Francisan Spirituality: Following St Francis Today*, London: SPCK.

Ramsey, Michael, 1972, *The Christian Priest Today*, London: SPCK.

Raworth, Kate, 2018, *Doughnut Economics: Seven Ways to Think Like a 21st Century Economist*, London: Random House.

Richardson, Alan and John Bowden (eds), 1983, *A New Dictionary of Christian Theology*, London: SCM Press.

Rilke, Rainer Maria, 2011, *Selected Poems*, Oxford World's Classics, Oxford: Oxford University Press.

Robson, Michael J. P. (ed.), 2012, *The Cambridge Companion to Francis of Assisi*, Cambridge: Cambridge University Press.

Rohr, Richard, OFM, 2014, *Eager to Love: The Alternative Way of Francis of Assisi*, London: Hodder and Stoughton.

Saggau, Elise, OSF (ed.), 2003, *Franciscans and Creation: What is Our Responsibility?*, Washington Theological Union Symposium Papers, CFIT-ESC-OFM Series No. 3, St Bonaventure, New York: The Franciscan Institute.

Sayers, Susan, 2019, *This? How Christians Respond to Climate Change*, Stowmarket: Kevin Mayhew.

Scott, David, 2014, *Beyond the Drift: New and Selected Poems*, Hexham: Bloodaxe.

Sheldrake, Philip, 2005, *The New SCM Dictionary of Christian Spirituality*, London: SCM Press.

Short, William J., OFM, 1999, *Poverty and Joy: The Franciscan Tradition*, London: Darton, Longman and Todd.

Snow, Stephen, 2019, *The Green Light*, Edale: Whitmore.

Society of Saint Francis: First Order, www.franciscans.org.uk (accessed 12.6.20).

_____, Second Order, https://oscfreeland.wordpress.com/.

_____, Third Order, https://tssf.org.uk/.

Sorrell, Roger D., 1988, *St Francis of Assisi and Nature: Tradition and Innovation in Western Christian Attitudes Toward the Environment*, Oxford: Oxford University Press.

Spencer, Nicholas and Robert White, 2007, *Christianity, Climate Change and Sustainable Living*, London: SPCK.

Sydenham Garden, www.sydenhamgarden.org.uk (accessed 7.5.20).

Taplin, Kim, 2008, *Walking Aloud: Rambles in the Cherwell Valley*, Charlbury: Wychwood Press.

Teresa of Avila, 1995, *The Interior Castle*, London: Fount.

Thompson, Augustine, 2012, *Francis of Assisi: A New Biography*, London: Cornell.

Torkington, David, 2011, *Wisdom from Franciscan Italy: The Primacy of Love*, Ropley: O-Books.

Tyndale, William, 1848, *Doctrinal Theses and Introductions to Different Portions of the Holy Scriptures*, Cambridge: Cambridge University Press.

Underhill, Evelyn (nd), *The Mystics of the Church*, London: James Clarke.

Vauchez, André, 2012, *Francis of Assisi: The Life and Afterlife of a Medieval Saint*, London: Yale University Press.

Ward, Benedicta, SLG, 1975, *The Sayings of the Desert Fathers: The Alphabetical Collection*, Kalamazoo, MI: Cistercian Publications.

Ward, Frances, 2020, *Like There's No Tomorrow: Climate Crisis, Eco-Anxiety and God*, Durham: Sacristy Press.

The Way of a Pilgrim, 1965, trans R. M. French, London: SPCK.

Welby, Justin, 2016, *Dethroning Mammon: Making Money Serve Grace*, London: Bloomsbury.

Williams, Rowan, 2007, *Tokens of Trust: An Introduction to Christian Belief*, Norwich: Canterbury Press.

———, 2012, *Address to the Synod of Bishops in Rome*, http://aoc 2013.brix.fatbeehive.com/articles.php/2645/archbishops-address-to-the-synod-of-bishops-in-rome (accessed 10.6.20).

Williams, Rowan Clare, 2003, *A Condition of Complete Simplicity: Franciscan Wisdom for Today's World*, Norwich: Canterbury Press.

Wirzba, Norman, 2018, *Food and Faith: A Theology of Eating*, Cambridge: Cambridge University Press.

Woodhouse, Patrick, 2015, *Life in the Psalms: Contemporary Meaning in Ancient Texts*, London: Bloomsbury.

Wroe, Anne, 2018, *Francis: A Life in Songs*, London, Jonathan Cape.